C000174006

Sprite and Midget

JONATHAN EDWARDS

The Crowood Press

First published in 2001 by
The Crowood Press Ltd
Ramsbury, Marlborough
Wiltshire SN8 2HR

British Library Cataloguing-in-Publication Data
A catalogue record for this book is available from the British Library.

ISBN 1 86126 470 4

Typeset and designed by Shane O'Dwyer, 18 Theobald Street, Swindon

Printed and bound in Singapore by Craft Print International Ltd

CONTENTS

SPRITE AND MIDGET: FAMILY LIFE

Autumn 1956	Project work on original Austin-Healey Sprite began
May 1958	Introduction of the 'Frogeye' ('Bugeye' in the USA) Austin-Healey Sprite. No MG Midget at this stage
May/June 1961	'Frogeye' assembly discontinued. Introduction of twin restyled models with conventional nose/squared-up tail, as Sprite Mk II/MG Midget I, with 948cc engine
October 1962	From this point, Sprite/Midget cars had 1,098cc engines and front disc brakes
March 1964	Introduction of Sprite III/Midget II, with more powerful 1,098cc engine, half-elliptic leaf-spring rear suspension, wind-up windows in doors, and deeper windscreen
October 1966	Introduction of Sprite IV/Midget III, with 1,275cc engine and 'convertible' type hood
October 1969	Changes for 1970 Model Year include facelift, Rostyle wheels, new decorative details
January 1971	Austin-Healey Sprite became Austin Sprite: no badging changes to MG Midget
July 1971	Austin Sprite finally discontinued: MG Midget continued
August 1971	Changes for 1972 Model Year, including round-style rear wheelarch shape
October 1974	Introduction of MG Midget 1500, with Triumph 1,493cc engine and all-synchromesh gearbox, plus polyurethane bumper style
Autumn 1976	Changes for 1977 Model Year include lead-free fuel-tolerant engine and catalyst for all North American markets
November 1979	MG Midget range finally discontinued

CHAPTER ONE

Introduction

T HIS story really began in the early 1950s, not at MG, not with Donald Healey, but at the headquarters of the new BMC (British Motor Corporation) at Longbridge in Birmingham. BMC had been formed in 1952 by the fusion of Austin and the Nuffield organization. Austin was Birmingham-based, while Nuffield centred on Cowley, near Oxford, the chairman of the group being the thrusting and ambitious Leonard Lord.

Pre-1952, MG had been the famous sports car marque, owned by the Nuffield organization, which made all its cars at Abingdon (south of Oxford). The Austin-Healey marque was invented by Lord at the end of that year. Lord swept up the 'Healey 100' prototype which Donald Healey had inspired, setting out to have it manufactured at Longbridge.

Although both Austin-Healey and MG came in for a lot of forced rationalization in the 1950s – the 2.6-litre Austin-Healey 100 relied on much Austin A90 running gear, while the 1.5-litre MG MGA used the new BMC-type B-Series engine and transmission assemblies – there was no immediate co-operation between the two. In fact, quite the reverse occurred, for the Healey was sold through the Austin dealer chain, while the MG was sold either through specialist dealers, or through Morris dealerships. Not that they really competed with each other, for the Healey 100 was considerably larger, faster and more expensive than the MGA – the *real* competition to both of them came from the 2-litre Triumph TR2/TR3 models.

Once Len Lord (who became Sir Leonard in 1954) got a grip on BMC, he set out to merge Austin and Nuffield as much as possible, though the two different marques of sports car were allowed to carry on unhindered for a time. Neither, of course, could go ahead with new projects until their masters approved them, so although both Syd Enever's people at MG and Donald Healey's team at Warwick, were both very talented, they were often frustrated by corporate inertia.

Although BMC was very successful with its small family cars in the mid-1950s – the Austin A30 and the Morris Minor both sold in record numbers in spite of competing head-to-head, with Austin and Morris dealerships sometimes glaring at each other across the pavement in the High Street – there

seemed to be little inclination to build small sports cars. This may have seemed surprising – MG, after all, had underpinned its reputation in the 1930s with a series of appealing little Midgets – but there might have been something personal behind it. Len Lord, after all, had been running Nuffield in the mid-1930s when MG had needed to be rationalized and its racing activities were closed down. Those were the days when the MG business never seemed to make much money, and perhaps he was wary of getting into the same corner again.

There was also the fact that Len Lord had stormed out of Nuffield in 1936, then moved in to 'The Austin' in 1938, and after the foundation of BMC he always seemed to favour that side of the business. In the early 1950s there were one or two half-hearted Longbridge attempts to design sporty versions of the A-Series-engined A30, though these always failed because there was no current sports car expertise on that site.

Nothing at all happened until 1956, by which time MG had ushered the new MGA into production, while Healey had re-engineered the original Austin-Healey 100 cars into the six-cylinder-engined 100-Six. Sir Leonard then called in Donald Healey to a meeting (significantly, he did not consult MG at all, this being a repeat of the old Austin-Nuffield rivalry): as Donald's son Geoff later wrote: 'Both men agreed that sports cars were becoming expensive ... Len Lord then commented that what we needed was a small, low-cost sports car to fill the gap left by the disappearance of the Austin Seven Nippy and Ulster models of pre-war fame.' Of course, there was no mention of the most recent cars to carry the 'Midget' name – the P-Series or T-Series models – for these had been from the 'rival' group, even though that group had now been absorbed!

Back at Warwick, Donald and Geoff soon decided what ought to be done, and set out to design and build prototypes.

BUILDING THE BONES

As far as the Healey team were concerned, they were only designing a new small Austin-Healey –

The original Sprite, launched in 1958, had headlamps fixed in the bonnet panel. No wonder this type was soon christened 'Frogeye' (or 'Bugeye' in the United States).

and it might not even be approved for quantity production. At this stage they did not know where any such new car would be assembled (though they assumed that it would be at Longbridge), and they certainly kept everything secret from MG. At no time did they expect that such a car would ever evolve into an MG model too.

Amazingly enough, at this particular time there were no small-engined series-production sports cars on the market. The flood of cars that followed in the 1960s (many of then, in fairness, produced in response to what the Healey family was about to do) had not even been thought of. Most importantly, there were no little Triumphs and no little sporting Fiats so the competition, such as it would become, did not exist.

With this in mind – and Donald Healey was never likely to pass up the chance of breaking into another market sector – a compact little two seater coded 'Q' (later, as an official BMC project, it would become ADO 13) began to take shape. With a great deal of support from BMC's design office at Longbridge, the team which had produced the original Austin-Healey got going again – Geoff Healey led them, Barrie Bilbie carried out chassis design work, and Gerry Coker did the body engineering.

Right from the start, a steel monocoque structure was chosen, designed around the new 948cc Austin A35 engine, gearbox, back axle and front suspension components; the only important Morris Minor 'building block' was the rack-and-pinion steering. To feed the rear chassis loads into the monocoque in the best possible way, the team chose to use cantilever quarter-elliptic leaf springs to link the axle to the tub.

Calling in every favour from their regular suppliers, the Healey Motor Co. Ltd had the very first prototype on the road early in 1957. BMC's managing director George Harriman saw it weeks later, and Sir Leonard approved it during February 1957 – it was only at this time that news of its existence leaked out to the people at the MG factory who, apparently, were not best pleased. It was typical of Sir Leonard's 'can do' attitude, in those post-Suez Crisis days, that he urged the new car into production in near record time, for April 1958.

There were many differences in detail between the first prototype and the car that made it to the showrooms. It was originally meant for assembly at Longbridge, on the A35 assembly line, and as first styled, it had layback headlamps on the bonnet panel. During 1957, however, BMC decided to make Abingdon the centre of all its sports car assembly operations. The Big Healey moved in from Longbridge in the autumn of that year, and the new small sports car started its life in Abingdon in 1958.

In the meantime, the car had gained a name – 'Sprite'. Originally seen on a Riley sports car of the 1930s, this title had most recently been used on a still-born Lanchester saloon, but a bit of discreet negotiation with Daimler (owners of Lanchester by this time) brought it back into the BMC stable. When the Sprite went on sale in mid-1958, it fitted in perfectly to BMC's growing list of sports cars, all of which were being assembled at Abingdon. This was the UK retail price line-up of that period:

Austin-Healey Sprite	948cc/43bhp	£669
MG MGA	1,489cc/72bhp	£996
MG MGA Twin-Cam	1,588cc/108bhp	£1,266
Austin-Healey 100-Six	2,639cc/117bhp	£1,227

From that moment, the Sprite (and its descendants) became a very important fixture at Abingdon, where factory facilities were often overcrowded in future years to satisfy demand for all these sports cars. However, what followed was not always a simple story.

First came the Austin-Healey Sprite in 1958, which reigned, on its own, until 1961. Then came the restyled Sprite and its 'kissing cousin', the MG Midget. For years, the two cars were built literally side by side on the same assembly lines, the same improvements being applied to both cars at the same time.

Sprite and Midget sales were equally matched until the late 1960s, but soon after British Leyland was formed in 1968, rationalization set in. The new corporation was already building the successful Triumph Spitfire on another site (in Coventry), and concluded that three brands were excessive.

First of all, Sprite export sales ended in 1969, and when Donald Healey's agreement with the company concluded at the end of 1970, the 'Austin-Healey' brand was dropped completely. In 1971, as what was effectively a 'run-out' model, a car called the Austin Sprite (which was nothing more than a rebadged Austin-Healey) was built until July 1971, but was only ever intended to be a stopgap.

The Midget then carried on alone at Abingdon (its sales never quite made up for the loss of the Sprite, though they held up well in North Ameri-

OPPOSITE PAGE

TOP: Between 1961 and 1974, the basic Midget style changed very little, but there was much detail change between the 1965-model Mk II (left) and the early-1970s 'round-arch' Mk III (right).

BOTTOM: Nose to nose, about eight years separate the (left) 1965 Midget from (right) its 1973 sister model. Detail style changes were legion, but the proportions did not alter.

ca), but from late 1974 further rationalization was needed for the car to meet US regulations. The well-liked (but old) A-Series engine could no longer cope so, accordingly, the Midget 1500 used a Triumph Spitfire engine – this being the first and only time an MG-badged car ever did that – and carried on until late 1979, when British Leyland's ruthless running down of Abingdon began.

MG enthusiasts tend to maintain that British Leyland was always anti-MG, but this does not seem to have been the case. Although big money was spent on the Triumph TR7 project, British Leyland managed (or mismanaged?) the decline of the Spitfire in exactly the same way as the Midget. As with the Midget, there was no serious attempt to develop a successor, and the old car was killed off less than a year after the last Midget was produced. From that day until 1995, there was no attempt to build a quantity-production, small sports car in the UK, and when that day dawned, the new car was an MG.

PRODUCTION		CALENDAR YEAR	
YEAR	SPRITE	MIDGET	TOTAL
1958	8,729		8,729
1959	21,566		21,566
1960	18,648		18,648
1961	10,064	7,656	20,348
1962	12,041	9,906	24,107
1963	8,852	7,625	18,709
1964	11,157	11,450	22,895
1965	8,882	9,162	18,044
1966	7,024	6,842	13,866
1967	6,895	7,854	14,749
1968	7,049	7,272	14,321
1969	6,136	12,965	19,101
1970	1,282	15,106	16,388
1971	1,022	16,469	17,491
1972		16,243	16,243
1973		14,048	14,048
1974		12,443	12,443
1975		14,478	14,478
1976		16,879	16,879
1977		14,329	14,329
1978		14,312	14,312
1979		9,778	9,778
TOTALS	129,347*	224,817*	361,472**

* Abingdon assembly: ** including Innocenti assembly

NB: Well over 15,000 Innocenti models, with unique body styles, were produced in Italy.

'Round arch' Midgets (foreground) were built only from late 1971 to late 1974, otherwise all other cars (1961–71, and 1500s from 1974 to 1979) had squared-off wheel arches.

OPPOSITE PAGE

TOP: Original 1958–61 Sprites had a rounded tail, with no exterior boot access ...

BOTTOM: ... but from 1961, and the launch of the Midget, the tail treatment was changed, and a separate boot lid was added. This is a 1500 of 1974–79.

THIS PAGE

ABOVE: The first Sprites had a cheap and cheerful facia panel ...

BELOW: ... but by the 1970s the facia/instrument panel was an altogether plusher, and better-equipped, affair.

TOP: From 1958 to 1974, all Sprites and Midgets were powered by one or other derivative of the famous BMC A-Series engine.

BOTTOM: The Midget 1500's engine was a Triumph unit, almost identical to that being used in the Spitfire 1500 of the same period.

CHAPTER TWO

Sprite Frogeye

1958 to 1961

THE long-running Sprite/Midget family, built for twenty-one years, evolved so far that the final MG Midget model bore little technical relation to the original Austin-Healey Sprite. In addition, the roots of the original Sprite – nowadays we might say its 'DNA' – were very different. The original car was not an MG, but an Austin-Healey, and instead of being engineered at Abingdon it was designed by the Donald Healey Motor Co. at Warwick.

The original car was born thanks to the success of the first Austin-Healey – the larger Austin A90-engined 100, which had founded the dynasty. Sir Leonard Lord, who had done that important overnight deal with Donald Healey in 1952 – the deal which invented the Austin-Healey brand – knew that the initial project had been a gamble, but had seen it pay off. Now he wanted to repeat the trick, but at a lower price level.

Once again, it was Sir Leonard Lord and Donald Healey who triggered the design and development process, though neither was the hands-on engineer who shaped the car. Sir Leonard was the tycoon, the

backer, and the man who signed off the deal, while Donald Healey was the inspiration – the *capo di capo* – behind the team who designed the car.

Designed quickly in the autumn/winter of 1956–57, the first car was merely coded as 'Q', and it was not until the Austin drawing office (at Longbridge) became involved at the production and release stage that it acquired an official BMC project code – ADO 13. Although the car would be assembled at the MG factory at Abingdon, the MG design team (led by Syd Enever) did not become involved until a very late stage, when only detail improvements could be included.

From the very beginning, the philosophy was clear. BMC wanted a simple, easy to build, cheap to sell two-seater sports car, where driving down the price was always more important than driving

The original Sprite, as revealed in 1958, had an unmistakable style, where the high-placed headlamps, let in to the bonnet panel, were uniquely positioned. The front bumper blade was an optional extra at first.

up the specification. This Austin-Healey – which did not acquire its proper name of 'Sprite' until the development programme had been going ahead for some time – was always intended to use as many existing BMC (mainly Austin) 'building blocks' as possible. In that way, not only would the total investment be limited, but the development time would be compressed.

The Healey team achieved all this, and more, not only sticking closely to their brief, but also managing to give the new two-seater a sporty, responsive feel, combined with a great deal of character. It was a car that sold itself better on the road than ever it needed to do in the showrooms.

STRUCTURE

With BMC's approval, Geoff Healey and Barrie Bilbie dispensed with a separate chassis, and designed a short, compact all-steel monocoque. The original Austin-Healey had moved halfway to this ideal, with a body structure welded to a chassis frame, but the new car had a no-compromise unit-construction shell. This was the first – the very first – sports car in the world to adopt such a layout.

Based on a rock-solid underpan, with massive box-section sills, cross members in front of the seats and a cross member behind the seats, with a solid bulkhead and footwell covers between the engine bay and the passenger compartment, the monocoque was intended to be stiff and torsionally rigid yet, at the same time, to be cheap and simple to make. There were several critical features:

◆ Instead of having a conventional front-end arrangement, there was a complete bonnet/front-end/inner and outer front wings assembly, which hinged at the bulkhead and lifted up like a monster opening its jaws. Except for access to the battery and (optional extra) heater/ventilator assemblies, which were just ahead of the bulkhead, this ensured easy access to the entire under-bonnet area.

◆ To keep the heavy stress-bearing sections as compact as possible, rear suspension was by cantilever, quarter-elliptic, leaf springs and (above them) two radius arms, all of which were tied down to the transverse bulkhead behind the seats.

◆ Although the rear-end shape was conventional enough, there was no exterior boot lid. Access to the spare wheel, and to the stowage volume, had

to be gained from the passenger compartment, by tilting the seats forwards and grovelling in the gloom.

◆ Healey's plan to fit lie-back headlamps in the bonnet panel had not survived the development period, so because of legal requirements over minimum heights, fixed lights in a rather startled position were used instead. This instantly gave the new car its nickname – 'Frogeye' in the UK, 'Bugeye' in North America.

This front-end style was controversial, and soon there was a choice of alternative glass-fibre (GRP) assemblies instead, with headlamps in a more conventional position at the corner of the wing. Perhaps the prettiest of all was that developed by John Sprinzel for the 'Sebring' Sprites, which raced and rallied.

Although most Frogeyes were delivered with a front bumper (which, in the opinion of some people, quite spoilt the lines of the car), this was actually an optional extra on UK market cars. A pair of vertical overriders, but no horizontal bars, were standard at the rear.

RUNNING GEAR

The engine on this original type was a 43bhp version of the existing Austin A35 A-Series power unit. In A35 form it had a single Zenith carburettor and produced 34bhp, the power increase having come by using twin SUs, a separate exhaust manifold and a different camshaft profile. Tuners

Healey had originally wanted to specify fold-back headlamps for the Sprite, but cost considerations ruled that out. British regulations meant that the lamps had to be at this height, which explains the rather 'startled' look.

Apart from a controversy over the style, the only drawback to the Sprite's headlamps was that such an installation encouraged rust to breed at panel and cut-out edges.

had already discovered that this engine could be boosted much further than this, for in Frogeye tune it was at once docile yet high-revving. It held no horrors for BMC mechanics, all round the world.

Except in detail, the four-speed gearbox was almost the same as that already being fitted to the A35, and came complete with a remote-control centre change, with a short and stubby gear lever. Because the A35 casing and internal gears were all retained, the bad news was that the intermediate ratios were rather widely spaced by sports car standards, so it was not long before the Donald Healey company had started to market close-ratio gears.

Although the single dry-plate clutch itself was small (the plate was only 6.25in (16cm) in diameter), compared with the A35 it had increased clamping loads, and was well up to the job. Unhappily, because of the construction and layout of the monocoque, it was not possible to remove the gearbox for work without withdrawing the entire engine/transmission forwards – which was a major operation.

The back axle was, basically, a Rubery Owen-manufactured A35 assembly, though with its own special final drive ratio (4.22:1), and with appropriate brackets welded to it, so that it could be fixed to the quarter-elliptic springs (lower) and radius arms (upper).

SUSPENSION, STEERING AND BRAKES

This area was a clever, and redeveloped, amalgam of A35 and Morris Minor 1000 components – a true case of 'parts bin' engineering. At the front, the coil-spring independent suspension from the Austin A35 was adopted complete, which meant that the Armstrong lever-arm hydraulic dampers also doubled as top wishbones. However, as this was a 1950 design (which would last until 1979), it required more periodic lubrication and greasing than modern sports car owners would have liked. There was no anti-roll

bar in the standard specification, though once again the Donald Healey company soon developed one as an accessory/motorsport fitment.

Right from the start, Healey decided that the A35 steering gear, a worm-type installation which incorporated no fewer than six ball joints (all of which could be expected to wear!), was not right, so a modified version of the Morris Minor 1000 rack-and-pinion assembly was chosen instead, though a special pair of steering arms was needed to make the steering match up to the A35 suspension.

Spring rates and damper settings, of course, were special to the Sprite.

At the rear, the quarter-elliptic springs were firmly rated, and had no fewer than fifteen leaves, while trailing/radius arms were parallel to them, and Armstrong-type lever-arm dampers were mounted slightly inboard. There was no sideways location, and some drivers complained of a bit of rear-end 'steering', but this was nonetheless a very effective, space-saving installation.

The wheels were pressed steel discs with perforations, looking rather like those being used on the current MGA, but having only a 13in diameter. They were *not* the same as those fitted to the A35, though the pitch circle diameter of the stud holes was identical. Centre-lock wire spoke wheels were not available when the car was built, but once again the Donald Healey company soon put them on sale as popular after-market options.

The brakes were manufactured by Lockheed, and had 7in (18in) drums all round, closely related to the BMC saloon car installations. Donald Healey's company soon developed a disc brake conversion, although discs would not be standardized on these cars until late 1962.

ELECTRICAL EQUIPMENT

As was typical for a BMC car of this period, here was a car kitted out with standard Lucas items from stem to stern – ignition equipment, dynamo (generator), starter motor, lights, tail lamps and all other ancillaries. (It was not that there was no alternative to Lucas, but if a manufacturer tried to choose some other component, such as a battery or a voltage regulator, the overall cost of the *rest* of the Lucas equipment would suddenly sky-rocket. A closed-shop? Some would say so.)

This system was entirely conventional – with a 43AH battery, a Type C39 PV2 dynamo and a M35 GI inertia starter motor and a DM2 PH4 distributor. Well-known to all BMC dealer service shops, these were easy to service and (sometimes) repair – Lucas was, for a while, known as the 'Prince of Darkness' among cynical American owners. Because these were so ubiquitous it means than many of them stayed in production beyond the end of the twentieth century to service classic-car needs.

COCKPIT AND TRIM

Because this was always meant to be a 'cheap and cheerful' car, the weather protection was basic, though effective. In the UK, the windscreen had toughened glass, though a laminated screen was an option and was standard in major export markets such as North America.

By the end of 1958, a lift-off glass fibre hardtop had become optional, this also being an area where after-market makers tried to muscle in on BMC's own act. Despite the body colour chosen, BMC hardtops were always painted in ivory white.

The doors themselves were hollow shells with useful storage bins inside and, when required, the side-screens ('side-curtains' in North America) could be bolted into place on their top edge; otherwise, the screens would be stowed away in a bag in the cavernous boot, where it was all too easy for them to get scratched.

Early soft-top cars had flimsy-looking side-curtains without any form of flap (which meant that it was impossible to make hand-signals), whereas hardtop cars came equipped with more robust-looking sliding-screen types; the latter were adopted as standard on *all* cars from the spring of 1960.

To add to the weather protection, a full tonneau cover was also available, held down by a series of Dzus and 'Lift-the-Dot' fasteners around the periphery of the cockpit opening.

The soft-top was of the 'build-it-yourself' variety, normally unattached to the structure. The folding tubular frame merely dropped into slots behind each door, the plastic soft-top roof then being laid over the top of the frame, and fixed to the top of the windscreen and to slots and fasteners around the rear of the cockpit. Many hardy owners saw it as a demonstration of their manhood to use such protection as little as possible.

The cockpit itself was simply furnished, and had two vinyl-covered bucket seats, though only that of the driver could be adjusted for reach to the steering wheel. Seat backs, as already stated, could be hinged forward to give access to the boot area, there being no other method of accessing this volume. The entire floor was covered by a moulded rubber mat (of which there was no cheaper alternative), though because these wore through rapidly, especially under the driver's heels, few of today's cars will have original mouldings. Many will have been upgraded to a later, more durable, carpet specification.

The facia/instrument display was simplicity itself – being a flat, vinyl-covered board with four circular instruments grouped ahead of the driver's eye (but behind a simple two-spoked plastic steering wheel), with the switch-gear, including a combined ignition/headlamps switch, being mounted in the centre.

These were the days when a heater was not provided as standard equipment, this having extremely simple push–pull knobs for the hot-water valve control. There was no provision for a radio, though plenty of space – owners usually mounted the receiver by cutting a suitable hole in the passenger side of the dashboard.

PRODUCTION

Body shell monocoques were pressed and welded together at the modern Pressed Steel factory at Swindon, using floorpans provided by John Thompson Motor Pressings of Wolverhampton, and were then rust-inhibited and painted at the BMC/Morris Motors complex at Cowley, before being transported to the MG factory at Abingdon for final assembly.

Because Abingdon was an assembly, rather than a manufacturing, plant, every other major component was trucked there from another site – engines from Longbridge, transmissions from other BMC factories in the Birmingham area, the rear axle from Rubery Owen, front suspension pieces from A35 suppliers, brakes from Lockheed of Leamington Spa, electrical kits from Joseph Lucas in Birmingham, instruments from Smiths

PRODUCTION	AUSTIN–HEALEY SPRITE MK I
DATES	March 1958–February 1961
CHASSIS NUMBERS	AN5 501–AN5 50116
PRODUCTION BREAK POINTS	AN5 34556, introduction of sliding side-screens
TOTAL PRODUCED	48,987

near Oxford and in the London area, along with trim items from all over the industry.

Unlike the contemporary (Abingdon-built) MGA, where the engine and all chassis pieces were bolted to the chassis frame before the separate body shell was dropped into place, Sprite assembly started at Abingdon with the body shell as the main 'jig' for everything else. The massive front assembly (bonnet/wings/valances) was not fitted at first, so that the combined engine/gearbox assembly could be fitted from the front, followed by suspension, radiator and other engine bay components. The front-end body assembly was not refitted until a very late stage.

After the car had rolled down to the end of the line (once the wheels had been added, movement was by Abingdon 'man-power' – pushing!), it was fired up, given a very short road test in the lanes outside the factory, and prepared for dispatch.

CAREER

Launched in 1958, the Frogeye Sprite immediately became an important member of the Abingdon sports car family, and sold very rapidly for three years. In 1959, for example, no fewer than 21,566 such cars (on average, that is, about 450 every working week) were assembled at Abingdon, of which 16,908 went to left-hand-drive export territories, mainly North America. This made it the

most numerous car on Abingdon's production lines during that period.

The original Sprite was so successful, in fact, that when BMC decided on a restyle for 1961, they also decided to phase in an MG version as well – this being the subject of the next section.

RIVALS – NO CONTEST

Because Sir Leonard Lord had spotted such a big gap in the market place, the original Sprite had no serious rivals when it was introduced. Any small sports cars that *were* on sale were expensive, hand-built and produced by small companies. For example, in 1958 – when the original Sprite cost £687 – the only small sports cars in British price lists were the motorcycle-engined Berkeley (£650/ 492cc), the Fairthorpe Electron Minor (£720) and the Turner (£863) – all of which had nastily finished GRP body shells and no dealer back-up.

Overseas (and particularly in the North American market) the Sprite had a totally clear run, for none of the above mentioned were sold in numbers, and there was, as yet, no competition from Fiat. Even when the new Fiat 1200 Cabriolet appeared in 1959, it was a larger-engined, heavier and considerably more expensive car.

It was a happy situation, on which BMC capitalized and on which they built continually – until the arrival of the Triumph Spitfire at the end of 1962.

AUSTIN-HEALEY SPRITE MK I

ENGINE

Layout	Four cylinder, in-line
Block material	Cast iron
Head material	Cast iron
Peak power	43bhp (net) @ 5,200rpm
Peak torque	52lb ft @ 3,300rpm
Bore	62.94mm
Stroke	76.2mm
Cubic capacity	948cc
Compression ratio	8.3:1

FUEL SUPPLY

Carburettors	SU constant vacuum
Type	2 × H1
Fuel pump	AC mechanical

ELECTRICAL

Earth	Positive
Battery	BT7A 12-volt
Generator	Lucas C39 PV2 dynamo
Starter motor	Lucas M35 GI

TRANSMISSION

Clutch	Single dry plate
Clutch diameter	6¼in (16cm)
Gearbox type	Manual, four-speed, no synchromesh on first gear
Internal ratios	4th: 1.00; 3rd: 1.412; 2nd: 2.374; 1st: 3.627; reverse: 4.664:1
Overall gear ratios	4th: 4.22; 3rd: 5.959; 2nd: 10.018; 1st: 15.306; reverse: 19.682:1
Optional close ratio 'box:	
Internal ratios	4th: 1.00; 3rd: 1.357; 2nd: 1.916; 1st: 3.2; reverse: 4.114:1
Overall gear ratios	4th: 4.22; 3rd: 5.727; 2nd: 8.086; 1st: 13.50; reverse: 17.361:1

BRAKES

Front, type	Lockheed drum, hydraulic
Front, size	7 × 1¼in
Rear, type	Lockheed drum, hydraulic
Rear, size	7 × 1¼in

STEERING

Type	Rack and pinion
Turns (L–to–L)	2.5

Turning circle	29ft (8.8m) approx. between kerbs

FRONT SUSPENSION

Type	Independent, coil springs, wishbones
Anti-roll bar	Optional extra from Healey Motor Co.
Dampers	Lever arm, hydraulic

REAR SUSPENSION

Type	Beam axle, cantilever quarter-elliptic leaf springs, twin radius arms
Anti-roll bar	None
Dampers	Lever arm, hydraulic

WHEELS AND TYRES

Wheel size	13in diameter, 3½in rim width
Optional wire wheels	13in diameter, 3½in rim width, from Healey Motor Co.
Tyres	Cross-ply
Tyre size	5.20-13in

CAPACITIES

Engine oil	6.9 pints
Gearbox oil	2.2 pints
Differential oil	1.75 pints
Cooling system	10 pints
Fuel tank	6 Imperial gallons

DIMENSIONS

Length (with front bumper)	11ft 5¼in (3,490mm)
Width	4ft 5in (1,350mm)
Height (unladen)	4ft 1¾in (1,260mm)
Wheelbase	6ft 8in (2,030mm)
Front track	3ft 9¾in (1,160mm)
Rear track	3ft 8¾in (1,140mm)
Ground clearance (unladen)	5in (127mm)
Weight (unladen)	1,328lb (602kg)

PERFORMANCE

0–60mph (0–97kph)	20.5sec
Top speed	86mph (138kph)
Standing ¼-mile	21.8sec
Overall fuel consumption	34mpg (8.3ltr/100km)
Typical fuel consumption	c.40mpg (c.7ltr/100km)

INSET: The Sprite badge (left) was simple, straightforward and would be unaltered throughout its life – except in 1971 when 'Austin', instead of 'Austin-Healey' cars were built for a time. The badge on the right appeared on the tail of the original cars.

No-one could remain indifferent to the appealing looks of the first Sprite, which looked so perky, and so cheeky, that it almost automatically brought a smile to one's face.

THIS PAGE

TOP: Many early Sprites were sold without front bumpers – owners, in any case, tended to remove them to save weight, or because they thought the styling to be better that way.

BOTTOM: To make the original car light and strong, Healey designed the Sprite without an exterior boot lid. Access to the spare wheel, and stowage for luggage, was by folding forward the seats in the cockpit itself.

OPPOSITE PAGE

TOP: The obvious caption here is: 'Open Wide!' – this showing the way that the entire front-end of the Sprite's bodywork lifted up to give access for service and repairs. Getting the battery out (from behind the engine), though, was an awkward job where strong arms helped.

BOTTOM: The original Sprite was built down to a price, but was effective nonetheless. All rear-facing lamps were standard Lucas issue, and those over-riders were all the protection offered at the rear. The radio aerial fitment on this car was an accessory.

Although the Sprite's cockpit was small (shall we say 'snug'?), there was easy access through wide doors. Note – oddments could be stored in door bins and the side curtains were removable.

The 1958–61 Sprite had a simple but well laid out cockpit. Because there were no drop windows in the doors, there was space for storage bins instead, and although the handbrake was not a 'fly-off' item, it was very efficient indeed, as driving test/gymkhana enthusiasts soon discovered.

OPPOSITE PAGE
Sprite owners only put up the all-weather equipment in *very* bad conditions. Many, including the author, preferred to drive around with the soft-top down and the side curtains stowed.

The original Sprite facia included the obligatory rev-counter and large speedometer ahead of the driver's eyes. Customers were encouraged to add extras to their cars, which explains the supplementary instrument panel hung under the centre of the facia of this car. The radio, when fitted, usually found a home ahead of the passenger's eyes, and most Sprites were treated to an accessory steering wheel (to replace this, the standard item).

A neat little touch was the use of 'A H' impressions in the nave plates fitted to Frogeye Sprite wheels.

CHAPTER THREE

Sprite II/Midget I

THE new Frogeye had only been on sale for a year when thoughts turned to a serious restyle – and to adding an 'MG' version to the range. It is worth re-emphasizing, at this stage, that there was never an MG version of the original Frogeye Sprite, not in any particular market, nor even on paper within BMC. Several factors encouraged the addition of an 'MG' derivative, to run alongside the Sprite:

♦ The Sprite was being assembled in the MG factory at Abingdon, so merely to keep the peace among managers and workforce it made sense to add in an 'MG' to that situation.

♦ MG dealers all over the world were already jealous of the new Sprite's success – especially in North America, where so many British sports car sales were being made, and where MG were already suffering an onslaught from the Triumph TR3A.

♦ BMC's planners thought that their new 'badge-engineering' policy – that of wringing every possible sale from one basic design by using different names and front-end styles, and by selling the cars through different networks – would work well. It had already succeeded for the Rootes Group (Hillman/Singer/Sunbeam), and it showed every sign of succeeding at BMC, where the new for 1959 Pininfarina-styled B-Series saloons had already gone on sale in five guises.

The first major style change, and the only one to affect the car's basic shape, came in 1961, when the Frogeye Sprite gave way to the Sprite Mk II, and when a new MG Midget (near-identical to the Sprite) was also launched. This particular Sprite was registered in 1962.

Because the style and construction of the original Frogeye had caused controversy (not to say inter-company jealousy), it was almost inevitable that a restyle for a new model would result in a more conventional type of sports car. For the usual investment reasons the same basic monocoque/running gear/suspension layout would have to be retained, but an entirely new skin style was authorized. Even so, it surely made no styling or practical sense to invite Healey to style a new front end, while at the same time asking the MG team to develop a new rear end! This, by the way, originally went ahead with strict instructions from Sir Leonard Lord that neither team had to consult the other!

Geoff Healey (Austin-Healey) and Syd Enever (MG) soon agreed to ignore this dictat, got together, and blended the two schemes. The fact is, however, that the new car really came together as the result of two only lightly-coordinated efforts. Two new near identical cars – ADO41 was to be called Austin-Healey Sprite Mk II, while ADO 47 was to become the new-generation MG Midget – were then developed, with most of the actual detail re-engineering taking place in the MG design offices at Abingdon.

The basic change was not only to the style, where a conventional front-end was chosen (no more vast, lift-up, bonnet/wings!), but to provide a conventional boot lid. In addition, though they were to be mechanical twins, the philosophy was to provide two similar, but different, equipment packages, that of the MG being slightly up-market and better-specified, which meant that the Midget was always slightly more expensive than the equivalent Sprite.

STRUCTURE

Although the chassis/monocoque did the same job as before – with independent front suspension mounted directly to the front 'chassis' legs, and quarter-elliptic leaf springs tied to the cross member behind the seats – there was a complete rearrangement of the outer structure and skin panels.

At the front, instead of the lift-up bonnet/front end of the Frogeye, there was a totally conventional layout of front wings, transverse front panels, and a wide but separate bonnet panel (which was still hinged at the passenger bulkhead). Instead of sitting perkily in the bonnet, the headlamps were moved to a conventional position at the front corners, at the front of the wings themselves.

At the rear, not only was the style squared up considerably from that of the Frogeye, but a separate, lockable, lift-up boot lid was provided. There was a much larger cut-out behind the seats (of what body engineers call the 'shroud' area), which allowed the floor behind the seats to be reshaped, and even for an optional 'rear seat' cushion to be available. In spite of this, there was still no metal panel between the passenger compartment and the boot area – a Vynide-covered trim panel was provided instead.

For the first time, safety-belt mounting points, weld-plates and reinforcements were provided, these being located to the rear of the inner sill panels, on the transmission tunnel, and high up on the inner wheel arch.

Except that vast polyurethane bumpers would be added from late 1974, the style and the structure introduced in 1961 would now be used on all future Sprites and Midgets.

RUNNING GEAR

The same basic engine, transmission and back axle were used on this new variety of car, as had sufficed for the Frogeye, except for the following:

◆ On the first cars, the 948cc engine was supplied in uprated, 46bhp, form, with a 9.0:1 compression ratio and larger-type SU carbs: except for badging and numbering, Sprite and Midget engines were totally identical.

◆ The gearbox casing and general layout were as before, though the new car was fitted with the previously optional close-ratio gears as standard. As before, the final drive ratio was 4.22:1.

Compared with the Frogeye, the Sprite Mk II had a longer and more angular front-end style, with a more angular rear style in which there was an exterior boot lid. Side curtains were retained – these would not disappear until the next Mark, in 1964.

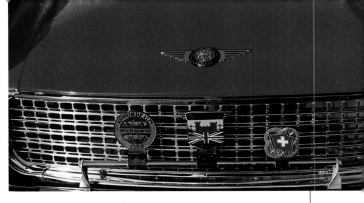

On the Mk II Sprite, there was a mesh grille and the Austin-Healey Sprite badge on the nose. The Midget had a different grille style with an 'MG' badge insert. Those badges on the grille of this car, of course, have been added by the owner.

CHANGES FROM LATE 1962

Starting in October 1962, a further uprated running gear package was standard. The A-Series engine was enlarged to 1,098cc (this, in fact, being the size of the engine also being specified for the new front-wheel-drive Morris 1100 at this time), which delivered no less than 56bhp and a most welcome matching increase in torque.

At the same time, a larger, 7in (18cm) diameter clutch was specified, bulk-ring synchromesh was adopted, reverse gear ratio was slightly altered, and the gearbox stiffness was increased by ribbing the main casing.

SUSPENSION, STEERING AND BRAKES

On the 948cc cars there was no basic change to suspension, steering or brakes compared with the Frogeye, the most significant updates being reserved for the arrival of the enlarged 1,098cc engine.

For the 1,098cc-engined cars, a new Lockheed assembly was specified, with 8.25in front discs matched to 7in diameter rear drums. This matched the car to the new opposition (the Triumph Spitfire!), and was much more powerful than before. The new disc brakes also meant that changes had to be made to the front suspension kingpost forgings.

A factory-fitted front suspension anti-roll bar kit became available from January 1964 (just before this model was withdrawn) – an option which would be carried over to future Sprite/Midget models.

Disc wheels became stronger (and non-ventilated) from the end of 1962, by which time a factory-fitted alternative of centre-lock, wire-spoke wheels with 4in rim widths had also become available: these were very popular, but were never standardized, for any market. It was not easy for a conversion to be carried out afterwards, for centre locks also required a package of different front discs and a slightly narrower rear-axle tube.

ELECTRICAL EQUIPMENT

Electrical changes were evolutionary, rather than revolutionary, with slightly different distributors for the latest 948cc, than for the 1,098cc engines. When the 1,098cc engine was standardized, the rev-counter became an electrical impulse (rather than cable driven), which allowed a Lucas C40-1 type of generator (with no cable drive) to be fitted.

Naturally, the restyle meant that headlamps, tail lamps (new clusters) and number-plate lamps had all been changed, although in most cases these all came from the Lucas 'parts bin'.

COCKPIT AND TRIM

The Midget could be distinguished from the Sprite, inside or outside, by the badging and decoration. The Sprite kept its original Frogeye badges, front and rear, had a plain mesh grille, and there was no extra decoration: 'AH' lettering was pressed into the wheel nave plates.

The Midget, on the other hand, carried an MG 'octagon' badge in a grille with vertical stripes, there were other octagons on the boot lid, in the centre of the facia and on the steering-wheel horn push, while there were chrome strips from front to rear of the bonnet and along the flanks (linking headlamps to tail lamps). The nave plates were plain.

A front bumper bar was standard on the Midget, and an optional extra on the Sprite (though most Sprites seem to have been built with them). On the Midget, there was a lockable T-handle on the boot lid, but an L-shaped handle on that of the Sprite.

Inside the car, the basic facia/instrument layout was like that of the Frogeye, though there had been minor repositioning of controls: both cars had rubber floor matting but carpet on the tunnel, and Midget seats were more plushly padded and trimmed than those of the Sprite; both Midget seats were adjustable, as were those of De Luxe Sprites. The door inners were more completely trimmed, still with stowage pockets, and the removable side-screens were the most robust yet designed at Abingdon.

Because of the way the rear of the cockpit floor had been redesigned, there was a carpeted near-flat shelf behind the seats, and a 'seat cushion' fitting for this area was available as an extra, although it was not very useful as leg room was nil.

The same 'build it yourself' soft-top was retained, though with the later Frogeye type of windscreen fastenings – and, of course, sliding panel side-screens were now standard on all models.

To match the new body style, and of course to match the much larger type of cockpit/shroud cut-out, BMC eventually standardized the option of a

All Austin-Healey Sprites built from 1958–70 had this distinctive front badge.

different, more voluminous and significantly more angular hardtop for both the Sprite and Midget types. Originally, the Sprite had a modified version of the original Frogeye type, but this was short-lived. Surprisingly few new cars seem to have been supplied with a hardtop.

PRODUCTION

The production process at Pressed Steel (body shells) and Cowley (paintwork) was much as before, though alterations had to be made at Abingdon to accommodate assembly of engine/gearbox assemblies to the revised body shell, where the front end and front wings were now welded into place.

As far as a production planner was concerned, the only difference between Sprites and Midgets was that they had to be painted in different colours (Cowley), trimmed with different detail colours (Abingdon), and fitted with their own distinctive badging and decoration (Abingdon).

Sprites and Midgets shared the same assembly-line facilities at Abingdon – the two types of cars being freely intermingled on the same tracks – and as before, the flow of engines, transmissions, suspensions, electrical kits and brakes all came from the same suppliers.

CAREER

The new cars were not launched together – the Sprite II bowed in early June 1961, the Midget four weeks later – but thereafter their careers ran strictly parallel to each other. Mechanically and structurally, the two cars were always equal, the same extras (though not the same colour/trim combinations) being available for both types.

As a reminder, in 1961 the Sprite II cost £641, the new Midget £670, that £29 difference being reflected in the Midget's slightly higher level of equipment.

Original cars had 46bhp/948cc engines and all-drum brakes, while from the autumn of 1962 this spec. was upgraded to 56bhp/1,098cc and a front disc brake installation. No fewer than 24,107 cars were produced in 1962 – this was an all-time record for these cars – with the Sprite always slightly out-selling the Midget. Except for the 1963 Model Year upgrade, there were no other major changes in three years. The new Sprite III/Midget II took over in March 1964.

RIVALS

Even in 1961, when the restyled BMC cars were put on sale, there was still no major business rival for these cars – though, of course, that would all change in the autumn of 1962 when Triumph introduced its new Spitfire.

In 1961 Britain's own glass-fibre bodied 'specials' were no nearer acceptance than before (the Berkeley had died anyway), and all the real opposition came from Italy. The Italian-made Innocenti

PRODUCTION	AUSTIN–HEALEY SPRITE MK II/MG MIDGET MK I		
DATES	February 1961–March 1964		
CHASSIS NUMBERS	SPRITE:	HAN6 101–HAN6 24731	
		HAN7 24732–HAN7 38828	
	MIDGET:	GAN1 101–GAN1 16183	
		GAN2 16184–GAN2 25787	
PRODUCTION BREAK POINTS	At introduction of HAN7/GAN2 sequence, 1,098cc engine and front wheel disc brakes		
TOTAL PRODUCED	31,665 Sprite; 25,681 Midget		

OPTIONS

COLOURS*

948CC MODELS

- ◆ Black
- ◆ Clipper Blue (Midget only)
- ◆ Ice Blue (Midget only)
- ◆ Iris Blue (Sprite only)
- ◆ Speedwell Blue
- ◆ Almond Green (Midget only)
- ◆ Dove Grey (Midget only)
- ◆ Farina Grey (Midget only)
- ◆ Deep Pink (Sprite only)
- ◆ Signal Red (Sprite only)
- ◆ Tartan Red (Midget only)
- ◆ Old English White
- ◆ Highway Yellow (Sprite only)

1098CC MODELS

- ◆ Black
- ◆ Ice Blue (Midget only)
- ◆ Iris Blue (Sprite only)
- ◆ British Racing Green
- ◆ Dove Grey
- ◆ Signal Red (Sprite only)
- ◆ Tartan Red (Midget only)
- ◆ Old English White
- ◆ Fiesta Yellow (Sprite only)

* Available for either car, unless noted

ACCESSORIES

- ◆ Heater
- ◆ Radio
- ◆ Fresh air unit (alternative to heater)
- ◆ Screen washers
- ◆ 6-ply tyres
- ◆ Whitewall tyres

- ◆ Wire-spoke wheels (1,098cc-engined cars only)
- ◆ Front anti-roll car kit (from January 1964)
- ◆ Laminated windscreen
- ◆ Tonneau cover
- ◆ Hardtop
- ◆ Locking petrol cap

At this time, BMC officially approved accessories included: windtone horns, luggage rack, fire extinguisher, reverse lamp, wing mirrors, child's seat, exhaust pipe trim, seat covers and other 'convenience' items.

In addition, the Donald Healey Motor Co. Ltd offered a whole range of performance-raising items, for the engine, transmission and suspension.

Spider – which was basically a rebodied Sprite – appeared in 1961, with the same running gear, but was a larger, heavier and somewhat more costly car. Except in Italy, in any case, it was no competition to the UK product, for production was limited to left-hand drive cars, and the only export territories officially served were Switzerland and the USA. Between 1961 and 1970, total production was only about 17,500 – an average of less than 2,000/year.

The Fiat Spider grew up a little in the early 1960s, although a 1.5-litre engine replaced the original 1.2-litre in 1963, putting it outside the Abingdon car's price and performance range. The Fiat sold steadily in the USA, but not as well as the Sprite/Midget.

The major competition, without question, came from the Triumph Spitfire, which was introduced in October 1962, just as the Sprite/Midget was uprated to its 1,098cc/front disc brakes spec. This was both wise *and* fortunate, for the Spitfire had both those features from the outset.

For the next eighteen years, the Spitfire and the Sprite/Midget would do battle, head to head, both in the showrooms and on the race track, with honours being even in all cases. 1963–64 Spitfires had 1.1-litre/63bhp engines, and sold for £641 in the UK, $2,199 in the USA, which was worryingly close to the Midget's package. Although the Triumph had independent rear suspension, this was swing axle, so it did not handle as well, but it was well-equipped (overdrive was optional – this never being offered on the Abingdon cars), and good-looking. Both cars sold extremely well in the USA, where it mattered.

SPRITE II/MIDGET I

29

AUSTIN-HEALEY SPRITE MK I / MG MIDGET MK I

(Figures for 1,098cc-engined examples in square brackets)

ENGINE

Layout	Four cylinder, in-line
Block material	Cast iron
Head material	Cast iron
Peak power	46bhp (net) @ 5,500rpm [56bhp (net) @ 5,500rpm]
Peak torque	53lb ft @ 3,000rpm [62 lb ft @3,250rpm]
Bore	62.94mm [64.5mm]
Stroke	76.2mm [83.72mm]
Cubic capacity	948cc [1,098cc]
Compression ratio	9.0:1 [8.9:1]

FUEL SUPPLY

Carburettors	SU constant vacuum
Type	$2 \times$ HS2
Fuel pump	AC mechanical

ELECTRICAL

Earth	Positive
Battery	BT7A 12-volt
Generator	Lucas C39 PV2 [C40-1] dynamo
Starter motor	Lucas M35 GI

TRANSMISSION

Clutch	Single dry plate
Clutch diameter	6¼in (16cm) [7¼in (18cm)]
Gearbox type	Manual, four-speed, no synchromesh on first gear
Internal ratios	4th: 1.00; 3rd: 1.357; 2nd: 1.916; 1st: 3.2; reverse: 4.114:1 [4.12:1]
Overall gear ratios	4th: 4.22; 3rd: 5.727; 2nd: 8.086; 1st: 13.50; reverse: 17361:1 [17.386:1]

BRAKES

Front, type	Lockheed drum, hydraulic [disc]
Front, size	7×1¼in [8¼in diameter]
Rear, type	Lockheed drum, hydraulic
Rear, size	7×1¼in

STEERING

Type	Rack and pinion
Turns (L–to–L)	2.5
Turning circle	29ft (8.8m) approx. between kerbs

FRONT SUSPENSION

Type	Independent, coil springs, wishbones
Anti-roll bar	Optional extra from Healey Motor Co. [from 1964, from factory]
Dampers	Lever arm, hydraulic

REAR SUSPENSION

Type	Beam axle, cantilever quarter-elliptic leaf springs, twin radius arms
Anti-roll bar	None
Dampers	Lever arm, hydraulic

WHEELS AND TYRES

Wheel size	13in diameter, 3.5in rim width
Optional wire wheels	13in diameter, from Healey Motor Co. [13in × 4in rim width, from factory, from late 1962]
Tyres	Cross-ply
Tyre size	5.20-13in

CAPACITIES

Engine oil	6.9 pints
Gearbox oil	2.2 pints
Differential oil	1.75 pints
Cooling system	10 pints
Fuel tank	6 Imperial gallons

DIMENSIONS

Length (with front bumper)	11ft 5.9in (3,500mm)
Width	4ft 5in (1,350mm)
Height (unladen)	4ft 1¾in (1,260mm)
Wheelbase	6ft 8in (2,030mm)
Front track	3ft 9¾in (1,160mm)
Rear track	3ft 8¾in (1,140mm)
Ground clearance (unladen)	5in (127mm)
Weight (unladen)	1,525lb (692kg)

PERFORMANCE

0–60mph (0–97kph)	20.0sec [16.9sec]
Top speed	86mph (138kph) [89mph (143kph)]
Standing ¼-mile	22.0sec [21.0sec]
Overall fuel consumption	39mpg (7.2ltr/100km) [30mpg (9.4ltr/100km)]
Typical fuel consumption	c.43mpg (c.7ltr/100km) [c.37mpg (c.7.6ltr/100km)]

Compared with the Frogeye, the front-end style of the Sprite Mk II was more conventional. This time round, the front-end sheet metal was all fixed to the monocoque, for engine bay access was now to be by a conventional lift-up bonnet.

THIS PAGE
From 1961, and original facelift time, all Sprites (and, of course, Midgets) had a conventional opening bonnet, which was hinged at the scuttle. Access for maintenance was not quite as ideal as that in the Frogeye but was still good enough for owner-drivers to carry out their own work.

OPPOSITE PAGE
TOP: Sprite Mk II and Midget Mk I were structurally and mechanically identical. Sprites (this car) had a simple mesh grille and the Austin-Healey badge on the nose: Midgets had a vertical radiator slat grille which included an MG badge and chrome strips along the flanks.

BOTTOM: Although the sheer 'cheekiness' of the original Frogeye was lost at restyle time, the new Sprite Mk II (which retained its cantilever quarter-elliptic suspension under the skin) was a very practical and versatile little sports car.

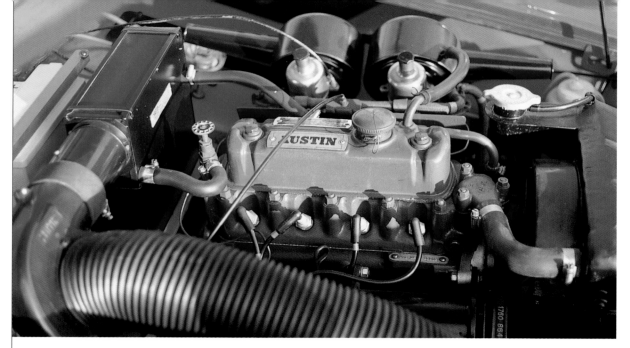

ABOVE: In 1961 the A-Series engine was a 46bhp 948cc unit, but from the autumn of 1962 it was enlarged to 56bhp and 1,098cc.

LEFT: As with the Frogeye, Mk II Sprites had wheel nave plates on which the 'A H' badge was stamped. In the case of the MG Midget, this identification was omitted.

BELOW: For Sprite Mk II/Midget I, there were no basic changes to the facia style from that of the Frogeye. This car has had a flexible accessory map light fitted for use in rallies. This was a Sprite II: on the Midget there would also be a padded crash roll above the facia and an MG badge in the centre of the steering wheel.

CHAPTER FOUR

Sprite III/Midget II

1964 to 1966

LESS than three years after the new Midget had first appeared, as a clone of the second type of Austin-Healey Sprite, it was time for another major change. Although they looked superficially the same, compared with the Sprite II/Midget I cars, in 1964 the Sprite III/Midget II models were a big leap forward, not least in chassis design and in equipment. As with the earlier cars, there were compelling reasons why this should be so. Now that both of BMC's sports car dealer chains were able to sell the same car, it had to be kept abreast of the new, and dangerous, rival – the Triumph Spitfire.

BMC had been shocked by the arrival of the Spitfire – although the Corporation knew it was coming, it was not prepared for the performance and equipment standards which were immediately offered. In 1963 and 1964 the Sprite/Midget cars lagged behind – and now, for a new iteration, this had to be rectified.

There was neither time nor spare investment capital, nor the man-hours, to indulge in a restyle, but there was time for many aspects of the design to be improved. Compared with the 1961–64 models, therefore, the Sprite III/Midget II offered the following important advances:

◆ A more powerful, more torquey and more robust 1,098cc engine.

◆ A new rear suspension, which would alter the handling characteristics.

◆ A much upgraded cockpit and interior with, among other details, wind-up door windows and a new facia layout.

From 1964, the family progressed to Sprite III/Midget II, where the visual differences were wind-up windows in the doors, a new and larger windscreen, and a reshaped soft-top to match. This is a 1965 Midget II, with optional wire wheels.

Amazingly, this was done without destroying the existing style, character or value for money. When the new cars were announced, they were only £24 more expensive than before – and still cheaper than the Spitfire. BMC, in fact, had a long-term masterplan for these cars, so this was merely another step in the improvement process. From late 1966, therefore, these cars would be ousted by yet more powerful versions.

STRUCTURE

All in all, in producing this new version, the MG design team had been very clever. The structural changes were out of sight, and one had to look closely to see that new doors and a totally different windscreen (windshield) had been fitted.

Structurally, there were two major updates – one to support a new rear suspension, the other to incorporate new doors and windscreen:

- Because the original cantilever quarter-elliptic leaf springs had been abandoned in favour of conventional half-elliptics (see the Suspension section), new 'chassis legs' were grafted into the existing structure – up and over the line of the rear axle – so that the half elliptic spring's rear hanger could be pivoted from a position just ahead of the tail lamps. Behind the seats, the cross-member layout was modified to suit – and though the original radius arms had been deleted, the lever-arm dampers kept to their old position.

- To accommodate wind-down windows, new door assemblies were designed, though these fitted into the same body shell apertures as before. There was a new and deeper windscreen, though this did not affect the main structure.

RUNNING GEAR

At first glance, the engine/transmission/back axle installation was as before, but each 'building block' had been updated:

- Although still of 1,098cc, the crankshaft of the latest engine was given increased (2in/50mm) main bearing diameters. This, a modified cylinder head casting with different port profiles and larger inlet valves,

plus revised inlet and exhaust manifolds, saw peak power rise to 59bhp at 5,750rpm. This was the lustiest Sprite/Midget engine so far.

This, incidentally, was the point at which an SU electric fuel pump took over from the AC mechanical pump used in earlier examples, and when closed-circuit crankcase breathing pipes were standardized.

To help keep engine temperatures in check when it was used hard, an oil cooler would become optional equipment from June 1965.

- Internally, the back axle design was not changed, but detail changes were made to the bracketry on the casing, to accommodate the half-elliptic leaf springs (which passed under the tubes), and to provide a different fixing for the shock-absorber linkage.

SUSPENSION, STEERING AND BRAKES

The major innovation was at the rear, where the cantilever quarter-elliptic springing of earlier models had been abandoned, along with the radius arms that were aligned above those springs.

In their place was a pair of conventional half-elliptic leaf-springs, which provided their own fore and aft location. The new springs, and the lever-arm damper settings that went with them, were arranged to give a rather softer ride than before. The new car handled in a more conventional manner – on earlier types there had been a suggestion

Centre-lock chrome-plated wire-spoke wheels were a very popular extra for Midgets and Sprites of this type.

of 'rear-end' steer, especially when radius arm bushes had begun to wear. The quarter-elliptics, too, had been prone to breaking leaves, which ceased to be a problem with the new cars.

Except in detail, no changes needed to be made to the front suspension, or to the rack and pinion steering gear, or indeed to the Lockheed brakes.

Standard wheel and tyre specifications were not changed (centre-lock wire-spoke wheels were optional extras), though this was the first Sprite/Midget on which factory-fitted radial-ply tyres (145-13in section) became available. In later, 'classic', years, almost all owners have specified radials, which not only improve the roadholding, but also offer increased tyre life.

ELECTRICAL EQUIPMENT

Compared with the model it replaced, there were only minor differences and updates in the Lucas electrical equipment, these changes mainly having to take account of the new facia layout, the use of an electric fuel pump and the standard fitting of an electric rev-counter. Although both innovations were sweeping the British industry, there was no sign of negative earth electrics, or of the use of an AC generator (alternator) being used – these would follow in the *next* model.

By this period in history, it is worth noting that several different markets demanded special attention to headlamps, the positions and types of other lamps, and high-tension electrical suppression. In 'classic' cars that may have been purchased in one country, then shipped to another, this might be important.

COCKPIT AND TRIM

Visually, and in terms of what used to be called 'showroom appeal', the biggest advance for the Sprite III/Midget II was in the style, layout, equipment and presentation of the cockpit and interior. This all centred around the use of wind-up windows (instead of detachable plastic side-screens), which brought the Sprite/Midget into line with other sports cars being built at Abingdon, and of course with the Triumph Spitfire. The improvements are best described as follows:

◆ Completely new passenger doors were provided, with wind-up window glass and with swivelling quarter windows ahead of them. At the same time, anti-burst interior door latches were provided, while the trim panel/stowage locker were pushed further inboard (leaving slightly reduced

elbow/shoulder room for the occupants).

To match this redesign, these became the first Sprite/Midget models to be equipped with push-button style exterior door handles and latches, and they were also the first Sprite/Midget types where the doors could be locked.

◆ To match the new wind-up windows and swivelling quarter lights, the windscreen was significantly deeper than before, was more robustly fixed to the body shell, and incorporated a chrome-plated centre tie-rod which provided height adjustment for the rear-view mirror.

◆ There was a brand new facia layout in black-crackle enamel, where the rev-counter and speedometer were angled inwards and slightly cowled on a 'panel within a panel'. Because this was not a full-width display, for the very first time there was space for a small parcel shelf ahead of the passenger.

To match this new style, there was a new type of sprung-three-spoke steering wheel, close in design to that of the current MGB, which was allied to a new steering column and the new self-cancelling indicator control stalk.

As before, for the Midget there were MG octagon badges on the wheel and in the middle of the facia, while the Sprite now enjoyed an Austin (not Austin-Healey) heraldic emblem in the centre of the wheel.

◆ Seats and carpeting, also, were upgraded, this being the first Sprite/Midget in which there was wall-to-wall carpeting on the floor, over the transmission tunnel and on the back shelf (for which an optional 'seat cushion' was still available).

The latest well-padded seat style looked much like that of the current MGB, the Sprite having benefited most of all by this upgrade.

Seat belts, of course, were still not compulsory fitments, but BMC dealers could (and often did) fit factory-developed static belts, for which the mounting points were still available.

◆ As before, a detachable glass-fibre hardtop (the same component, in fact,

PRODUCTION — AUSTIN–HEALEY SPRITE MK III/MG MIDGET MK II

DATES	January 1964–November 1967
CHASSIS NUMBERS	SPRITE: HAN8–38854–HAN8 64734 (YHGN8 and … 9 types available in Australia to November 1967)
	MIDGET: GAN3 25825–GAN3 52389
PRODUCTION BREAK POINTS	Longer front springs fitted, January 1966 for North America, March 1966, all markets
TOTAL PRODUCED	25,905 Sprites; 26,601 Midgets

as on the previous model) was available. In the UK, in 1964, its retail cost was £48.33. Many customers, however, chose to purchase the optional tonneau cover instead (it only cost £5.44). The latest cover came complete with three zip fasteners – one down the centre of the car and two running inwards from the line of the B-post (rear of the door opening) towards the centre of the car.

◆ A full-width front bumper was now standard on all types.

PRODUCTION

The rhythm of assembly carried on much as it had done with earlier types. Now that Abingdon had turned to building monocoque MGBs instead of separate-chassis MGAs, production methods for Sprite/Midgets/MGBs and Austin-Healey 3000s were all much the same, with painted and partly trimmed cars arriving regularly by transporter and with all the major components and sub-assemblies also flooding on – either from other BMC factories (engines and transmissions, for instance), or direct from suppliers.

Compared with previous models, Abingdon was also sending even more part-complete chassis (to Innocenti, for completion as Spiders), or CKD packs (now exclusively left-hand drive, in contrast to the previous models). All seasons were busy, but in the spring the pace became frenetic. In 1964, no fewer than 21,361 cars of both types were built – and sometimes this meant that 500 cars were leaving the gates of Abingdon in a single week, of which nearly 300 would be going to North America.

CAREER

Although this was the second, and in chassis terms, a major upheaval compared with what had gone before, the Sprite III/Midget II had a short life. In truth, however, this was not because it was not a success, but because it was laying the foundations for even more capable derivatives – the Sprite IV/Midget III – which were to follow.

Assembly began at Abingdon early in 1964, with the public introduction following in March. On this occasion, the Sprite and Midget types were launched together, with no attempt to differentiate between the two badges (which was quite a different approach to that used with the previous car). UK prices were closer than ever, with the Sprite being listed at £611 and the Midget at £623 – a difference of a mere £12.

The twin cars sold very well, right from the start (more were actually built in 1964 than in either of the seasons that followed). With this evolution of the cars, the Sprite always sold almost car-to-car with the Midget – 25,905 compared with 26,601, in fact – though there was no attempt to rationalize selling and marketing techniques in any territory.

Except for the usual steady introduction of minor improvements, there were no major updates during the 1964–66 period, and production ended abruptly in September 1966, to make way for the next derivative, the 1,275cc-engined types.

RIVALS

In this relatively short period – only 2½ years, including three summer 'selling seasons' – the Sprite/Midget still had only one major rival throughout, the Triumph Spitfire. For the future, however, the BMC sports cars would also have to worry about two widely different newcomers – the rear-engined Fiat 850 Spider which made its bow in 1965, and the high-revving twin-cam Honda S800 which went on sale in export territories in 1966.

As with the earlier BMC models, the Spitfire was a serious rival, because it matched the Abingdon cars in performance and price, and had a similar, no-nonsense, two-seater/open sports car image. The launch of the Midget II/Sprite III clawed back the Spitfire's original performance and equipment advantage, but the Spitfire II of 1965 was more powerful (67bhp) than before. In 1964, in the UK, a Sprite III cost £611, a Midget II £623 and a Spitfire £641. As before, the Spitfire sold equally as well as the Abingdon cars.

Compared with the British cars, the Bertone-styled Fiat 850 Spider was not as well-equipped, nor did it handle as well, but it was quite fast – 92mph (148kmh). The good news for BMC was that it was quite expensive in the UK – £1,000 – and sold at a similar premium in the USA.

The Honda S800 was an enigma. Its engine was a twin-cam jewel – only 791cc, but 70bhp – and with a top speed of 94mph (151kmh) it was equal to either of the Abingdon cars. But in 1966 it cost £779, the interior was cramped and the handling was not up to scratch. Nevertheless, it *might* become a serious threat in the USA in the future.

No mistaking the make of car here, this being one of the definite ways in which BMC delineated the MG Midget from the basically similar Austin-Healey Sprite of this period.

OPTIONS	Available for either car, unless noted	COLOURS

◆ Black (Midget only)	◆ Tartan Red
◆ Riviera Blue	◆ Old English White
◆ British Racing Green	◆ Fiesta Yellow (Sprite only)
◆ Dove Grey	◆ Highway Yellow (Sprite only)

ACCESSORIES

◆ Heater	◆ Front anti-roll car kit
◆ Fresh air unit (alternative to heater)	◆ Laminated windscreen
◆ Radio	◆ Tonneau cover kit
◆ 6-ply tyres	◆ Hardtop
◆ Whitewall tyres	◆ Engine oil cooler
◆ Dunlop radial-ply tyres (145-13)	◆ Locking petrol cap
◆ Wire-spoke wheels	◆ Rear compartment seat cushion

At this time, BMC officially approved accessories included: windtone horns, luggage rack, fire extinguisher, reverse lamp, wing mirrors, child's seat, exhaust pipe trim, seat covers and other 'convenience' items.

In addition, the BMC Competitions Department offered a whole range of performance-raising items, for the engine, transmission and suspension.

AUSTIN-HEALEY SPRITE MK III/MG MIDGET MK II

ENGINE

Layout	Four cylinder, in line
Block material	Cast iron
Head material	Cast iron
Peak power	59bhp (net) @ 5,750rpm
Peak torque	65lb.ft @ 3,500rpm
Bore	64.58mm
Stroke	83.72mm
Cubic capacity	1,098cc
Compression ratio	8.9:1

FUEL SUPPLY

Carburettors	SU constant vacuum
Type	2 × HS2
Fuel pump	SU electric

ELECTRICAL

Earth	Positive
Battery	N9 12-volt
Generator	Lucas C40-1 dynamo
Starter motor	Lucas M35 GI

TRANSMISSION

Clutch	Single dry plate
Clutch diameter	7¼in
Gearbox type	Manual, four-speed, no synchromesh on first gear
Internal ratios	4th: 1.00; 3rd: 1.357; 2nd: 1.916; 1st: 3.2; reverse: 4.12:1
Overall gear ratios	4th: 4.22; 3rd: 5.727; 2nd: 8.086; 1st: 13.50; reverse: 17.386:1

BRAKES

Front, type	Lockheed disc, hydraulic
Front, size	8¼in diameter
Rear, type	Lockheed drum, hydraulic
Rear, size	7 × 1.25in

STEERING

Type	Rack and pinion
Turns (L–to–L)	2.5
Turning circle	29ft (8.8m) approx. between kerbs

FRONT SUSPENSION

Type	Independent, coil springs, wishbones
Anti-roll bar	Optional extra
Dampers	Lever arm, hydraulic

REAR SUSPENSION

Type	Beam axle, half-elliptic leaf springs
Anti-roll bar	None
Dampers	Lever arm, hydraulic

WHEELS AND TYRES

Wheel size	13in diameter, 3.5in rim width
Optional wire wheels	13in × 4.0in rim width
Tyres	Cross-ply, optional 145-13in radial-ply
Tyre size	5.20-13in

CAPACITIES

Engine oil	6.9 pints
Gearbox oil	2.2 pints
Differential oil	1.75 pints
Cooling system	10 pints
Fuel tank	6 Imperial gallons

DIMENSIONS

Length (with front bumper)	11ft 5.9in (3,500mm)
Width	4ft 5in (1,350mm)
Height (unladen)	4ft 1¾in (1,260mm)
Wheelbase	6ft 8in (2,030mm
Front track	3ft 9¾in (1,160mm)
Rear track	3ft 8¾in (1,140mm)
Ground clearance (unladen)	5in (127mm)
Weight (unladen)	1,566lb (710kg)

PERFORMANCE

0–60mph (0–97kph)	16.9sec
Top speed	92mph (148kmh)
Standing ¼-mile	19.7sec
Overall fuel consumption	29mpg (9.6ltr/100km)
Typical fuel consumption	c.32mpg (c.8.8ltr/100km)

From this angle on the Midget II, the new door skins (to accommodate wind-up windows), the deeper screen and the exterior door handles are all useful recognition points. The centre-lock wire wheels were extras, and were very popular fittings.

ABOVE: From 1964, the Sprite/Midget family reached its near-definitive shape, for there would be no further basic change of proportions until the arrival of black bumpers at the end of 1974.

BELOW: From this angle, the only way to identify an MG from a Austin-Healey derivative of the 1964–1966 models was to look at the badging (and see that MGs had chrome strips along their flanks). From this angle, the close resemblance to the larger MGB is startling.

TOP: When the Sprite III/Midget II model appeared in 1964, one of the new features was a smarter, restyled facia/instrument panel. The alloy-spoked steering wheel on this car is a period accessory fitment.

BOTTOM: Sprite III/Midget II models used 59bhp 1,098cc A-Series engines. This particular car, photographed in the 1990s, seems to have been fitted with a gold-painted replacement power unit. The bulky plastic tube is feeding fresh air to the heater unit on the scuttle.

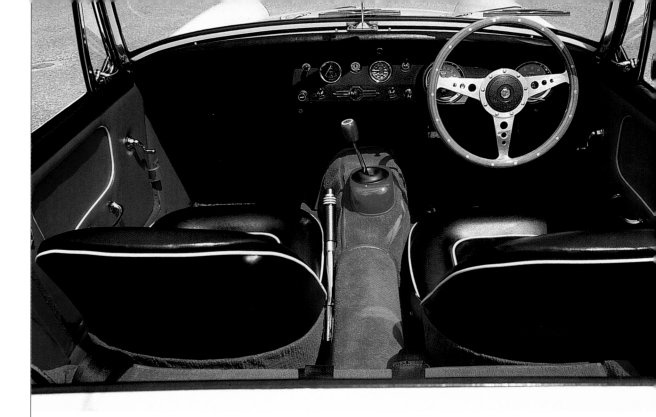

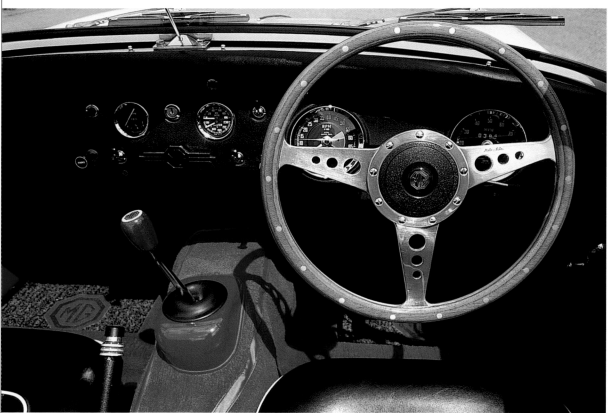

TOP: The Sprite III/Midget II cars (this is a Midget) had a new and neatly styled display of instruments, and from this view the smaller door stowage pockets are also obvious. This particular steering wheel is non-standard.

ABOVE: The proud owner of this 1965 Midget II has not only fitted an alloy-spoked accessory steering wheel, but he has also added floor carpets which carry the MG logo. Sprite/MG owners, at this price level, were always encouraged to customize their cars in this way.

From spring 1964, with wind-up windows in the doors, swivelling quarter windows were also standardized. The seats were much as before, and although there was space behind the seats, BMC never seriously intended it for carrying even occasional passengers.

The driving compartment of all such Sprites and Midgets was none too large, for the steering wheel (an accessory, in this case) was quite close to the seat cushion. Owners' Manuals were important documents (many owners did their own maintenance on what was a simple car) – and have been reprinted by specialist Austin-Healey and MG car clubs in later years.

RIGHT: The only way to differentiate an MG from an Austin-Healey of this type was to inspect the badge in the centre of the facia panel. On this car, the MG-badged wooden gear lever knob is an accessory.

SPRITE III \ MIDGET II

ABOVE: Like the Mk II Sprite of 1961–64, the Sprite III of 1964–66 was always provided with this simple badge in the centre of the boot lid. This, of course, was a different style of badge from that fitted to Frogeye types.

RIGHT: The MG octagon and the 'Midget' label below it was used on these cars until 1974, though there was no 'Midget' badge on the final 1500 models.

Neat, wind-cheating and useful, but not standard – this was a typical sort of wing mirror sold by 'speed equipment' and accessory shops at the time.

CHAPTER FIVE

Sprite IV/Midget III

1966 to 1974

IN October 1966, BMC announced a new matching pair of Sprites and Midgets – the Mk IV and Mk III respectively – these being a mature reworking of everything towards which Healey at Warwick and MG at Abingdon had been working for so long. At last, it seemed, the engine could match the potential of the chassis, the chassis itself need make no excuses (nor plead cost restrictions to excuse shortcomings), the style was acceptable all round the world – and the cars were still a complete match for their opposition.

The new cars looked almost exactly like those that they superseded, for all the novelty was under the bonnet at first and inside the cabin. At last – more than two years after it had first been seen in the appealing little Mini-Cooper S – a 1,275cc version of the A-Series engine had been adopted (though it was not as highly tuned as in the front-wheel-drive car). It was the sturdiest engine yet used in a Sprite/Midget, finally giving it the best possible capacity for use in 1.3-litre category motorsport.

If Leyland had not merged with BMC in 1968 to form British Leyland, these cars would surely not have carried on for eight full years – nor is it likely that the Austin-Healey brand would have disappeared so rapidly. Unhappily, what was placarded as sensible rationalization (but was more closely related to 'not invented here' jealousy) saw export sales of Sprites end in the summer of 1969, the Austin-Healey brand killed off at the end of 1970, and a very half-hearted attempt (as the 'Austin Sprite') taking over for seven months in 1971.

Although Midget Mk IIIs, introduced in late 1966, looked basically as before, the visual style differences soon piled up. By 1970 the Midget had lost its decorative chrome striping, both on the bonnet and along the flanks. These wheels were standard Midget/Sprite fittings for 1970 and 1971 Model Years.

British Leyland, on the other hand, authorized expensive technical work to keep the cars abreast of ever-changing North American legislation, agreed a mid-life cosmetic facelift for 1970, and also allowed the introduction of the 'round-wheel arch' style at the end of 1971. The fact that the cars' engineering began to lag behind that of their main rivals in the 1970s was neither ignored, nor was it voluntary, for the dead hand of corporate politics leaned more and more heavily on what Abingdon was allowed to do.

In later, 'classic', years, these cars – particularly those with the round-arch style – would become the most popular, and valuable, of all Sprite/Midget types.

STRUCTURE

Experience had shown that the latest chassis/hull structure, complete with half-elliptic leaf springs at the rear, was a solid, safe, mass, so until the round-arch style was introduced for 1972, changes and improvements to the pressed-steel body/chassis unit were kept down to a minimum.

From the start, the most noticeable difference was that the cockpit opening had been lengthened behind the seats, to allow for a fold-down soft-top to be installed, this having involved a new pressing ('shroud') ahead of the boot lid. However, once North American crash-test requirements demanded these, a series of stiffening measures were applied to accept an energy-absorbing steering column, different bonnet hinges and a three-wiper spindle set-up. This was the time when side and reverse lamps tended to move around, and when side repeater lights (for the USA) also arrived – but the basic shell was little changed.

From October 1971, what is always known as the 'round-wheel arch' style was introduced. This featured a change to the rear (but not the front) wheel cut-out shape, which also necessitated a different inner-wheel arch pressing too. At the end of this car's life, however, the shell was still very close to that which appeared in 1966.

RUNNING GEAR

For the Sprite IV/Midget III, the big update was to the engine, where the sturdier 1,275cc engine (larger cylinder bore, but *shorter* stroke) took over from the 1,098cc engine – there being no untidy overlaps or exceptions.

Not only was this done to provide the new derivatives with more power and torque (peak power was up by 10 per cent, while peak torque rose by an encouraging 11 per cent), but to provide more potential for further power tuning. Although the sports cars did not have every feature of the rather specialized Mini-Cooper S power units (the cylinder heads were different, and the Midget had a different camshaft profile), they shared the same stiffer cylinder block and the same breathing potential.

In the next few years, particularly because of the impact of tighter exhaust emission regulations in North America, there were several different engine sub-types involving different carburettor settings, high-pressure air injection to exhaust manifolds, evaporative fuel loss controls – and modified fuel tanks to suit. Regrettably, there is no space here to list all the details.

In the transmission, a 6.5in (16.5cm) diameter diaphragm spring clutch took over from the traditional single dry plate/coil spring variety, though the gearbox itself was not changed, the internal ratios being the same as before. At first, the final drive ratio was 4.22:1, as on the older model, which was then changed to 3.9:1 from December 1968 production.

SUSPENSION, STEERING AND BRAKES

Since all the hard work and detail redevelopment had been done with the previous model – the change over to half-elliptic leaf springs had given development engineers time to retune sporting and damper rates – there were virtually no changes at first when the 1,275cc-engined cars were announced.

The front suspension was totally unchanged at first, then there was a slight increase in the free length of the front coil springs from August 1972 (this made a marginal difference to the ride height), and then from August 1973 (just in time for what we might call the beginning of '1974 Model Year') the optional anti-roll bar was standardized. Although the rear leaf springs were slightly harder-rated than before, otherwise there were absolutely no changes to the rear suspension.

There was no immediate change to the steering gear, but due to the effects of North American safety legislation, from January 1968 cars for that market were fitted with energy-absorbing steering columns, and from the end of 1968 there was also a new padded rim steering wheel with a different spoke pattern. From October 1971, UK market cars also gained a simpler type of collapsible column along with the steering lock mechanism that had become compulsory. (This was not the last steering wheel, by the way, for there would be two further changes before 1974, when the model was displaced by the Midget 1500.)

The first signs of inter-marque rationalization then followed in January 1972, when a Triumph-sourced rack and pinion steering gear was fitted: this was slightly lower-geared than before. The change, in any case, was probably inevitable, for the Morris Minor 1000 that had donated the previous system had finally gone out of production in 1971.

Important specification changes to the braking system were mainly confined to fitting a dual-circuit installation on cars produced for the North American market.

Wheel specifications came in for several changes. At first, there was the choice of steel disc, or centre-lock wire-spoke – both being to the previous model's specification. Then, from late 169, to coincide with the facelift for 1970 Model Year (the start of HAN10/GAN5 chassis numbers), the plain steel wheel was dropped in favour of 4.5J x 13in Rostyle steel wheels.

This wheel, which had eight rectangular cooling slots, lasted only two years – for when the round-arch style was introduced, a more conventional Rostyle wheel, with four prominent and bright-finish spokes, was fitted instead. This was the point, too, where 145-13in radial-ply tyres became standard equipment.

No shortage of 'MG' badges on a Midget III – Cecil Kimber, MG's founder, would have been proud of that.

ELECTRICAL EQUIPMENT

Those contemplating restoration of a Sprite/Midget of this model should note that there was one major change, dating from late 1967 (and the start-up of North American specification models), when the entire electrical system changed from positive to negative earth. This move, of course, affected many of the other fittings, including instruments.

At first, the Lucas 'kit' was carried over *en bloc* from the previous model – which is to say that there was a C40 direct current dynamo, an M35G starter and an RB106 control box. Alternators

were soon to be available at the right price, these being fitted to Australian market cars from mid-1969: a 16ACR (later 17ACR) arrived for other markets from December 1972.

Particularly for North American market cars, this was also a period when all manner of extra detail lamps, buzzers, repeaters and warning lights were standardized. In most cases, these were not fitted to home market machines.

STYLE CHANGES

Style changes were small, but persistent, through the eight-year life of the car.

- ◆ Original 1967 MY cars looked exactly the same as the last of the Sprite III/Midget II models.

- ◆ From October 1969, the cars underwent a facelift, becoming visually identical except for their badging. There was no longer an 'Austin-Healey' or 'MG' front grille – both cars had the same black inset style, which was based on the earlier Sprite pressing.

   Part of this package was the use of 'Version 1' Rostyle steel wheels, black-painted sills, slimmer bumpers and 'Sprite' or 'Midget' badges on those sills behind the front-wheel cut-outs. British Leyland roundels were fitted towards the rear of the front wings (ahead of the windscreen pillar), this fitting being reduced to one passenger-side roundel from spring 1972, and on early cars there were black-painted windscreen pillars (though this move was soon reversed).

   This was the point at which the Midget finally lost its extra brightwork.

- ◆ From January 1971, the Austin-Healey brand was dropped, though for seven months an otherwise identical car that was badged 'Austin Sprite' was built. After that, only the MG Midget remained.

- ◆ From October 1971, the round-wheel arch body style took over, at which point 'Version 2' Rostyle wheels took over, this style then continuing unchanged until October 1974, when the Midget III was replaced by the Midget 1500.

◆ From December 1973 (American market cars only), big rubber over-riders were fitted to front and rear bumpers, the better to meet the latest crash-test regulations.

COCKPIT AND TRIM

The main change in and around the cockpit was that this was the first Sprite/Midget for which there was a permanently fixed, foldaway, soft-top hood and frame arrangement. Because of the geometry of its folding, when being furled, it meant that the cockpit rim had to be moved backwards by four inches. When erected, the side-on profile of this new layout was slightly lower than before, and suited the body shell very well. This installation worked well, and would not need to be changed again in the life of the car.

As before, the alternative to the soft-top was to invest in a removable hardtop, which was unavoidably different from the Sprite III/Midget II component, though the style, complete with separate quarter window, was the same as before.

The rather ridiculous 'rear seat cushion' option was discontinued from the end of the 1969 Model Year (that is, at 'facelift time'), and at this point there were several minor changes to trim styles, patterns and colours. The recesses inside the doors (which were useful for stowage) were finally deleted at 'round-arch' introduction time, after which the only place left for stowage was the small parcel shelf ahead of the passenger's knees.

In the UK, the fitting of seat belts to new cars (but *not* the wearing of them), became compulsory from 1 January 1968, this task initially being carried out at dealerships during pre-delivery work. Factory-fitted belts became usual from January 1971. Although the familiar facia/instrument panel of Sprite III/Midget II cars was carried over, complete, until late 1967, from that point the North American-specification left-hand drive cars were given an entirely fresh style, with instruments grouped behind the steering wheel, a heavily padded roll across the top of the panel and toggle switches for the first time on these cars. From 1968, this completely differentiated North American from the other specification cars, a situation which would continue to the end of the Midget's days in 1979.

PRODUCTION

As ever, the production process was concentrated at Abingdon, though because there was a problem with engine supply at first, deliveries were slow to start, which also explains why a limited number

Who needs to say anything more? Annoyingly, though, low life all round the world tend to use a screwdriver to get those for 'souvenirs'. If you are in the market for a Midget, always make sure that the front grille is intact!

of cars (489 Austin-Healeys and 476 Midgets) were assembled at Cowley from January to March 1967, to help clear the backlog. This was a 'one-off' situation that was not repeated.

BMC hid the fact that late-1966 production (due to a shortage of 1,275cc engines) was so limited, for only 406 new-model Sprites and 359 Midgets were built in the final months of the year – with export deliveries not properly getting under way until the first months of 1967.

By 1968 (and even though the North American specification cars were more complicated to build) annual production was up to 14,321; after the Sprite model was withdrawn this would increase to 16,243 cars in 1972.

Detailed analysis of Abingdon production shows that Sprite exports ceased completely at the end of 1969, and that Midget exports to countries *other* than North America soon dropped significantly in the early 1970s. In 1972, for example, all but ninety-two export cars went to North America, and after that *every* exported Midget went to North America.

It is worth noting that because Austin-Healey 3000 series production ended in 1967, from 1968 onwards the only cars being assembled at Abingdon were Sprite/Midget and MGB/MGC models, which must have simplified the planning, ordering and scheduling process considerably.

CAREER

With a life spanning eight years, during which all manner of cosmetic and detail technical updates were applied, these cars were the longest-running of all Sprite/Midget types. In eight years – October 1966 to October 1974 – no fewer than 123,036 cars were built, of which 48,287 were the still-fashionable 'round-wheel arch' variety.

Taken month by month, this was a logical eight years, usually in response to new marketing requirements, or another raft of regulations beaming in from across the Atlantic, though hindsight now shows up a myriad of changes which occurred during that time. The headline changes were as indicated in the box (*right*).

RIVALS

Not only was this a period when the cars from Abingdon carried on their head-to-head contest with the Triumph Spitfire, but it was also when Fiat redoubled their efforts to produce a worthy competitor. For BMC/British Leyland, at least, there was still no sign that the Japanese could – or would – try to muscle in.

OCTOBER 1966: Start of Sprite IV/Midget III production.
LATE 1967: First production of special North American specification cars, new facia, and so on.
OCTOBER 1969: Introduction of facelift models. End of Sprite exports.
DECEMBER 1970: 'Austin-Healey Sprite' model dropped.
JANUARY 1971: Introduction of 'Austin Sprite'.
JULY 1971: End of short-lived 'Austin Sprite' assembly. Thereafter, only the 'MG Midget' would be built.
LATE 1971: Introduction of the 'round-wheel arch' style.
OCTOBER 1974: End of Midget III assembly, in favour of new Midget 1500.

As already pointed out, after the Austin-Healey and MG brands came under the umbrella of British Leyland in 1968, they found themselves having to be in rather uneasy 'co-operation' with Triumph, the two plants being separated by 50 miles of Midlands real estate and several generations of design philosophy. Internal rivalries,

PRODUCTION	AUSTIN–HEALEY SPRITE MK IV/MG MIDGET MK III/AUSTIN SPRITE	
DATES	October 1966–October 1974	
CHASSIS NUMBERS	SPRITE:	HAN9 38854–HAN9 85286
		HAN10 85410–HAN10 86802
	AUSTIN SPRITE:	AAN10 86803–AAN10 87824
	MIDGET:	GAN4 52390–GAN4 74885
		GAN5 74886–GAN5 153920
PRODUCTION BREAKPOINTS	January–March 1967: some cars produced at Cowley	
	November 1967: First special North American market types produced	
	November 1967: Change to negative earth electrics	
	December 1968: Cosmetic facelift for 1969 Model Year	
	September 1969: Cosmetic facelift for 1970 Model Year, and to HAN10/GAN5 chassis numbers	
	October 1971: Start-up of round rear wheel arch body style production	
TOTAL PRODUCED	21,768 Austin-Healey Sprite; 1,022 Austin Sprite; 100,246 Midget	

however, became simpler after mid-1971, for this was when the Sprite model was killed off, to give the Midget a clear run in its battle with the Spitfire.

This was never going to be easy, though, as Triumph kept a wary eye on whatever Abingdon was doing (internally, and confidentially, they tried to second-guess Abingdon, though this was not encouraged) and tried to match it. Further, they seemed to attract investment spending at a level never granted to Abingdon.

In 1967, the Spitfire became the Mk 3, complete with 75bhp/1.3-litres; in 1970 it became the Mk IV with a neat styling update and a much-improved rear suspension, being then sold in the USA with a punchier 1.5-litre engine during the early 1970s. Throughout this time the Triumph carried on outselling the Midget around the world (although *not* in North America), and Midget prices were always lower.

The Midget could always outsell the rear-engined Fiat 850 Spider of the late 1960s, but in late 1972 the arrival of its replacement, the Fiat X1/9, was a real worry, for here was an advanced little two-seater (which the Midget was no longer). Complete with a mid-mounted 1.3-litre overhead-camshaft engine, a Bertone-styled structure, and all-round independent suspension, it was technically promising. Abingdon could only hope that it would be as rust-prone as all previous Fiats had been – which it was!

OPTIONS

COLOURS

- Aconite
- Aqua
- Black
- Basilica Blue
- Bedouin
- Blaze
- Bracken
- Midnight Blue
- Mineral Blue
- Royale Blue
- Teal Blue
- Harvest Gold
- British Racing Green
- Mallard Green

- New Racing Green
- Limeflower
- Mirage
- Damask Red
- Flame Red
- Tartan Red
- Black Tulip
- Tundra
- Glacier White
- Old English White
- Snowberry White
- Citron Yellow
- Pale Primrose (Yellow)
- Bronze Yellow

ACCESSORIES

- Heater
- Fresh air unit
  (alternative to heater)
- Radio
- Whitewall tyres
- Radial ply tyres (145-13)
  (standard from 1971)
- Wire-spoke wheels

- Front anti-roll car kit
  (standard on home market cars from 1973)
- Laminated windscreen
- Tonneau cover kit
- Hardtop
- Engine oil cooler
- Locking petrol cap
- Rear compartment seat cushion

At this time, BMC officially approved accessories included: windtone horns, luggage rack, fire extinguisher, reverse lamp, wing mirrors, child's seat, exhaust pipe trim, seat covers and other 'convenience' items.

In addition, the BMC Competitions Department/BMC Special Tuning offered a whole range of performance-raising items, for the engine, transmission and suspension.

AUSTIN-HEALEY SPRITE MK IV/MG MIDGET MK III/AUSTIN SPRITE

ENGINE

Layout	Four cylinder, in-line
Block material	Cast iron
Head material	Cast iron
Peak power	65bhp (net) @ 6,000rpm
Peak torque	72lb.ft @ 3,000rpm
Bore	70.61mm
Stroke	81.28mm
Cubic capacity	1,275cc
Compression ratio	8.8:1

FUEL SUPPLY

Carburettors	SU constant vacuum
Type	2 × HS2
Fuel pump	SU electric

ELECTRICAL

Earth	Positive (negative from Nov. 1967)
Battery	N9 12-volt
Generator	Lucas C40-1 dynamo (alternator, progressively, from April 1969)

STARTER MOTOR

Lucas M35 GI

TRANSMISSION

Clutch	Single-plate diaphragm spring
Clutch diameter	6½in (16.5cm)
Gearbox type	Manual, four-speed, no synchromesh on first gear
Internal ratios	4th: 1.00; 3rd: 1.357; 2nd: 1.916; 1st: 3.2; reverse: 4.12:1

1966 TO DECEMBER 1968

Overall gear ratios	4th: 4.22; 3rd: 5.727; 2nd: 8.086; 1st: 13.50; reverse: 17.386:1

FROM DECEMBER 1968

Overall gear ratios	4th: 3.9; 3rd: 5.292; 2nd: 7.472, 1st: 12.48; reverse: 16.068

BRAKES

Front, type	Lockheed disc, hydraulic
Front, size	8.25in diameter
Rear, type	Lockheed drum, hydraulic
Rear, size	7 × 1¼in

STEERING

Type	Rack and pinion
Turns (L-to-L)	2.5

Turning circle — 29ft (8.8m) approx. between kerbs

FRONT SUSPENSION

Type	Independent, coil springs, wishbones
Anti-roll bar	Optional extra (standard from August 1973, home market)
Dampers	Lever arm, hydraulic

REAR SUSPENSION

Type springs	Beam axle, half-elliptic leaf
Anti-roll bar	None
Dampers	Lever arm, hydraulic

WHEELS AND TYRES

Wheel size	3in diameter, 3½in rim width (4½in rims from start of HAN10/GAN5)
Optional wire wheels	13in × 4.0in rim width
Tyres	Cross-ply, optional 145-13in radial-ply, standard radial-plys for 1972 MY and later
Tyre size	5.20-13in (145-13in radials from 1972)

CAPACITIES

Engine oil	6.9 pints
Gearbox oil	2.2 pints
Differential oil	1.75 pints
Cooling system	10 pints
Fuel tank	6 Imperial gallons

DIMENSIONS

Length (with front bumper)	11ft 5.9in (3,500mm)
Width	4ft 5in (1,350mm)
Height (unladen)	4ft 1¾in (1,260mm)
Wheelbase	6ft 8in (2,030mm)
Front track	3ft 9¾in (1,160mm)
Rear track	3ft 8¾in (1,140mm)
Ground clearance (unladen)	5in (127mm)
Weight (unladen)	1,575lb (714kg)

PERFORMANCE

0–60mph (0–97kph)	14.6sec
Top speed	94mph (150kph)
Standing ¼-mile	19.7sec
Overall fuel consumption	28mpg (10ltr/100km)
Typical fuel consumption	c.30mpg (c.9.4ltr/100km)

Quarter bumpers, square-pattern number plate and flat-style lamp clusters identify this car as a 'facelift' car, built from late 1969.

From October 1971 (effectively, for MY 1972 and beyond) the body style of the Midget was modified to what is now known as the 'round-arch' rear wheel arch style. This was done purely for appearance purposes, and was very popular. Earlier Midget III/Sprite IVs had used the earlier-type squared-off arch cut-out.

TOP: This Midget III, dating from 1971–72, not only features the round-arch shape of rear wing pressing, but the owner has fitted an accessory (non-factory) roll-hoop to protect the occupants in the case of an accident. By this point, the Sprite derivatives had been discontinued, and there was much less decoration on the outside of the shell than heretofore.

ABOVE: This Midget Mk III of 1972 shows off the accessory roll-hoop fitted by a later owner, and it also confirms that the basic proportions of the body were the same as they had been on the first Midgets.

ABOVE: Rostyle wheels of this type were standardized on the Midget at the same time as the round-arch body style was phased in, and would stay with the Midget until production ended in 1979. Maybe it is not obvious here, but there was also a new type of fold-down soft-top assembly on this Mark, and a soft-top cover was standard, the rear body shell cut-out having been extended rearwards to allow for this.

There was no basic facia change from Mk II Midget to Mk III Midget (this car), though this was yet another type of steering wheel, of which the Midget carried several types during its life.

For the Sprite Mk IV, and the Midget Mk III, the A-Series engine was enlarged to 1,275cc, which was exactly the same size as that of the Mini-Cooper S, though for the Abingdon-built sports car it was detuned and very different in detail. Externally, and when visually compared with the ousted 1,098cc engine, there were very few changes, as the SU carbs and the twin air cleaners took up the same stance as before.

On the Midget Mk III, as on early types, there was plenty of space around the engine bay for the owner to carry out maintenance and service on the A-Series engine. It was a simple matter, too, to remove the bonnet panel completely.

TOP: The Midget was always a well-proportioned little sports car, and in this early-1970s form it looked good from any angle. Except for the black bumpers that would follow in late 1974, in almost every way this was the definitive Midget shape of the 1970s.

BOTTOM: Because the Midget had only limited ground clearance, and a flat bottom to its structure, the exhaust system could look vulnerable, but if the driver took care when traversing rough roads (or, in later years, when traversing 'sleeping policemen') it was rarely damaged.

ABOVE: The twin driving lamps on this car are accessory fitments, otherwise this early 1970s Mk III looks much the same way as it would have done when it left Abingdon in 1972–73. The brightwork-detailed Rostyle wheels set off the paintwork perfectly.

BELOW: 'British Leyland' corporate badges (as seen here on the front wings, behind the front wheel arch cut-outs) were only fitted to Midgets between late 1969 and 1974. Many owners, who did not like the idea of MG being subservient to this industrial colossus, had them removed.

THIS PAGE

ABOVE: By 1973, when this Midget III was built, decoration (and identification) was at its simplest, for at the front the MG badge was built into the centre of the grille, and there was no brightwork on the bonnet. The driving lamps on this car are accessory extras.

This car, though more than twenty years old when photographed, was nicely maintained. Those Rostyle wheels, in particular, were prone to minor parking and 'kerbing' damage, and restoration could be time-consuming.

OPPOSITE PAGE

TOP: Almost every component of a Midget III of this period can still be bought, if restoration and repairs are needed. Because it is such a large pressing, getting the correct fitting (and panel gaps) between the bonnet and the front wings can be problematical.

BOTTOM: From the rear end, the styling detail of the Midget III was very pleasing, the identification of the car being made clear by the single badge (no 'Midget' on this type) on the boot lid.

OPPOSITE PAGE
On this Mk III, both the luggage grid and the 'Midget' badge have been added by the owner since it was sold to him. The 'Midget' badge had been discontinued from the standard specification at the end of the 1969 Model Year.

THIS PAGE
TOP: British Leyland, which had controlled MG since 1968, was determined to have this car *and* its owners identified from kerbside, with the name badge on the sill (which was painted in contrasting colour), and by the British Leyland roundel on the front wing itself.

BOTTOM: The owner of this 1973 Midget III has kept it looking as good as new for many years. Every fitting is as authentic now as it was when the car was assembled.

OPPOSITE PAGE

TOP: Easy to restore? Looks simple on this immaculately presented car, but in fact there are a number of different steel pressings involved around this corner of the shell, and corrosion around those side and headlamp housings could become a problem.

BOTTOM: On the boot lid of a Midget Mk III, original cars had the MG octagon and the 'Midget' badge, but the 'Midget' lettering was discontinued from late 1969 production. The luggage rack on this particular car is an accessory.

THIS PAGE

RIGHT: The swivelling quarter window and the door mirror on this car are standard, but that is an extra, auxiliary, panel of instruments bolted underneath the facia.

The round-arch style was short-lived, for it was only included on Midget IIIs built between late 1971 and the end of 'chrome bumper' assembly in late 1974.

LEFT: The door handle and separate lock arrangements on Midget IIIs were simple enough, but corrosion could easily start in the body cut-outs for both items, and after prolonged use the recess under the handle tends to collect scratches.

BMC/British Leyland dealers stocked a wide range of accessories for cars like the Midget in the early 1970s – this chrome-plated luggage rack being one of them.

ABOVE: Head restraints were fitted to North American market cars from December 1968, could soon be ordered as extras on UK market cars, and soon became standard. The windscreen surround, which had been black on earlier Mk IIIs, became bright again for 1970 and later models.

RIGHT: Many different steering wheels were fitted to Midget Mk IIIs over the years, some with holes in the spokes, some with slots and some with solid spokes! All, however, had MG badges on their horn push – this wheel, in fact, being an accessory extra.

BELOW: Details of the 'Midget' and 'British Leyland' roundels fitted to Midget Mk IIIs.

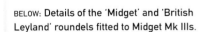

The chrome fitting under the MG badge is a cockpit illumination lamp. Please note, too, that rocker switches were fitted to the familiar facia on home market Midgets from the end of 1971.

As the years passed, Midget seats tended to become more bulky as cushioning was added, so the space inside the 1970s cockpits was always very snug and 'two-seater only'. Compared with earlier types, the door trim of a Midget III was much more 'finished' than ever before, but there were no door bins for stowage.

TOP: As on earlier Midgets, engine bay access was excellent.

BOTTOM: On the BMC A-Series engine, carburation and manifolding was all one side of the car (the left side, in Midgets) with all the engine electrical fittings – plugs, distributor, starter motor and generator – on the opposite side.

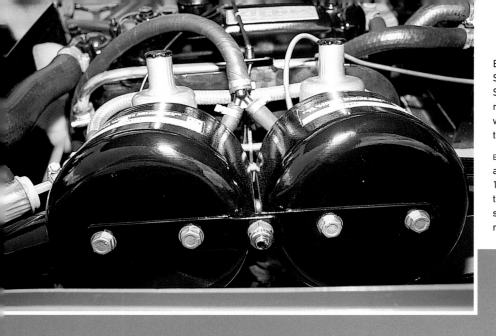

By the early 1970s, the once-simple SU carburettor installation of Sprite/Midget types was becoming more complex, for crankcase fumes were now being recycled through tubes, to help cut down on pollution.

BELOW: This Dorset-based Sprite was a race-modified Mk IV of the late 1960s/early 1970s. Depending on the regulatory limits that applied, such cars could be formidable, high-revving, class-winning two-seaters.

With race cars, it is best to suspend belief over dates and origins. The registration number suggests 1977–78, but the body shell suggests pre-1972, and the grille is Sprite (pre-1971), though there is an MG octagon on the boot! Whatever, the engine is 1,275cc A-Series, and very tuneable for motorsport.

This race-modified Mk IV Sprite has extra rubber straps to hold down the boot lid, a safety fuel tank has been fitted with a relocated filler neck and there is a sturdy roll cage inside the cabin.

The engine bay of this race-modified Sprite might be in less than concours condition, but the carburettors have special air filters, and there is a (compulsory-fitting) oil catch tank on the bulkhead close to the battery.

CHAPTER SIX

Midget 1500

IN October 1974, British Leyland astonished the MG fraternity. Not only did they inflict massive black polyurethane bumpers on the Midget (and the MGB, for that matter), but they re-equipped the car with a Triumph engine!

At the time, this caused such a storm that the real, pragmatic reasons were often obscured. In later years, too, classic MG enthusiasts stirred up dissent along the 'how could they?' lines, suggesting that, from within British Leyland, this was Triumph's way of killing off a rival marque.

This was all vicious hot air, and it is time that the various myths were laid to rest. The vast bumpers arrived because, between them, MG engineers and British Leyland stylists found it the only way to meet the latest in North American crash-test regulations without ruining the cars'

looks completely. The Triumph engine transplant was made simply because the venerable old BMC A-Series could no longer cope in North America – and the Spitfire unit could.

Whatever, the Midget 1500 was a car that might never have been developed if Midget sales to North America had not been so important. Important? Vital, more likely, because at this time, 75 to 80 per cent of all Midget production was of cars destined for sale in the USA and Canada. If the Midget should become uncompetitive in North America, its sales would collapse and the model would have to be scrapped.

MG, no doubt, would have liked to have seen new generation sports cars on sale by the 1970s, but a combination of British Leyland policy, investment constraints, North American legislation

The Midget 1500 was a major revision to the theme, not only with a different 1.5-litre engine, but with vast polyurethane bumpers to satisfy North American crash-test regulations. This is one of the last stream of Midgets to be produced in 1978–79.

and the first energy crisis all ensured that this could not be done.

Midget 1500s were to be built from September 1974 to December 1979, after which the car whose ancestors had started life more than twenty-one years earlier was finally discontinued.

STRUCTURE

At first glance, the big black bumpers were merely bolted on to the existing structure of the Mk III with one principal change – a reversion to the square-style wheel arches (which gave better crash-test performance). However, this was not in fact the case.

For the Midget 1500, there were extra stiffener sections linking the bulkhead with the front panel assembly, additional stiffener rails featuring under the rear floor, reinforcements in the shell to assist the rigid mountings of the new bumpers and new jacking points at the rear of the sills. Changes were also made to the transmission tunnel pressings, not only to accommodate the new all-synchromesh transmission, but to give access to the propeller shaft driving flange.

As before, North American market cars had other unique details such as the fixings for three (not two) windscreen wipers, cantilever bonnet hinges, burst-proof door catches and other such details. These were carried over from late-model Midget IIIs.

The bumpers – they were moulded in polyurethane, incidentally, not in 'rubber' as is sometimes written – concealed a sturdy steel armature inside the moulding, and at the front the style was such that it was no longer necessary to include a separate grille.

All these changes, plus the added complication of engine 'add-ons', imposed a weight penalty of no less than 57kg (125lb) to the unladen weight of the car. The car also rode slightly higher than before (once again, this was to meet North American legislation). At the front of the car, this was achieved by modifying the cross members, and at the rear by re-cambering the half-elliptic leaf springs.

Once modified, the structure did not need to be change again throughout the run of the model, so there is a very close relationship between the 1974–75 and 1979–80 models.

RUNNING GEAR

For the first and only time in the entire life of the Sprite/Midget family, when the Midget 1500 took over from the Mk III, there was a complete upheaval. Out went the long-running BMC A-Series engine and transmission, and in came a Triumph Spitfire 1500 engine, and an all-synchromesh gearbox which was derived from that used in the Morris Marina, and was itself a close relative of the Spitfire installation.

The engine change was not inspired by inter-company political spite, but because the old A-Series engine was finally at the end of its development life and could not be modified to deal with the unleaded fuel/exhaust catalyst regulations that were coming up on the horizon. Because the development and testing costs were high, luckily for British Leyland the Spitfire unit (which was equally venerable, had also started life at 803cc and had a three-bearing crankshaft) could, and would, fit into the Midget engine bay.

Visually, the two engines were completely different, for the Spitfire engine was rather bulkier (this explains why it could be stretched to a full 1.5 litres), and its carburettors were on the other (right) side of the engine. Although of the same 1,493cc type as used in the Spitfire 1500 (which was announced at the same time), the Midget 1500 used a different exhaust manifold. Although the UK peak power was almost the same as for the last A-Series engine in the Midget III, the Triumph engine seemed to give better results, for this was now a 100mph car – the only Midget ever to achieve three figures.

This was the period, incidentally, when engines tuned to meet US regulations suffered badly. All cars were fitted merely with a single Zenith–Stromberg carburettor instead of twin SUs. This, along with other power-choking fittings, meant that a mere 57bhp was produced – some sources quoting only 50bhp – the performance being reduced accordingly.

No changes, externally, to the door lock/key lock arrangements of the Midget 1500, but North American safety regulations influenced the use of anti-burst locking arrangements under the skin.

Midget 1500s were first fitted with exhaust catalysts from March 1975 (Californian market only), then from October 1975 all North American market specification cars were fitted with them. This expensive item (which had to be changed at 25,000-mile intervals) was never, however, fitted to UK market cars.

Fitting the all-synchromesh Marina gearbox was a definite advance for the Midget (it was the first and only derivative to do away with a 'crash' first gear), this being mated to the engine via a 7.25in (18.5cm) diameter diaphragm spring clutch. Because of its relationship to the Spitfire box, an overdrive option would have been feasible, but more expense would have been incurred in altering floorpan pressings to make space for this, so it was never offered in the Midget.

The rear axle of the 1500 was of the same type as used in all previous Midgets and Sprites (in historical terms, it dated back to the Austin A35 of the late 1950s!), and the only important change made during the life of the 1500 was that the final drive ratio was raised from 3.9:1 to 3.7:1 in August 1977, a move which made the car that important bit more high geared. Remember that the final drive ratio of the *original* Sprites and Midgets had been 4.22:1.

SUSPENSION, STEERING AND BRAKES

Although the Midget 1500 had a slightly bigger ride height (so that the new bumpers were at the best level to meet North American crash-test regulations), no major suspension changes had been needed to make this possible.

At the front, this was achieved by retaining the same geometry, wishbones and components, while making changes to the front cross member that supported them all. There was also a slightly longer front coil spring to add to the effect. (Interestingly enough, British Leyland's official dimensions for ride height and ground clearance do not reflect this increase, though it was definitely there …!)

The anti-roll bar, which had been standardized for UK market cars in 1973, was retained, but for North America the bar remained as an option until the start-up of 1978 Model Year cars. At the rear, a matching increase in the right height was achieved by fitting new, re-profiled, six-leaf half-elliptic springs, although compared with other Midgets there were no other changes.

The Triumph-sourced rack and pinion steering gear fitted to 'round-arch' cars of 1972–74 was retained for all Midget 1500s, though once again the advance of legislation meant that there would be two new types of collapsible steering columns (one 'energy absorbing' for North America, the other 'non-energy-absorbing' for the UK market).

It goes without saying that there were more changes to the steering wheels specs. For North America, from August 1977 there was a new type of four-spoke wheel (visually similar to that used in MGBs of the same vintage), along with decorative changes to the home market wheel.

There were two significant changes to the braking and wheels specifications: dual-circuit brakes were added to the UK specification from May 1978, which made this fitting the same as that on North American models. The centre-lock wire-spoke wheel option was withdrawn from UK market cars from mid-1976, though it continued, to the end, for North America.

ELECTRICAL EQUIPMENT

The electrical equipment of the 1500 followed on from that of the Mk III, except that the use of the Triumph engine meant that different components were needed in the engine bay. The 1,493cc Triumph engine carried all its electrical gear on the left side of the engine bay (the opposite side from the A-Series unit). The same Lucas ACR alternator was retained, as was an M35J starter.

COCKPIT AND TRIM

The major trim update, of course, was exterior, with the adoption of the large black polyurethane bumpers, but the cockpit and furnishings were changed only in detail from 1974 to 1979. The octagon MG badge appeared on the front of the front bumper and, as ever, a brightwork octagon was to be found in the centre of the boot lid, ahead of the handle. On most cars this was silver, but on some 1975 models ('Jubilee' year) it was gold.

Interestingly enough, the British Leyland roundel on the front wing was standard when the 1500 was announced, but was withdrawn at an unspecified point during the five-year career of the cars. Surely British Leyland was not now ashamed of itself?

Compared with the Mk III, there were virtually no changes to trim patterns, facia layout or the style. The UK market steering wheel was now a three-spoke style with spoke recesses but no perforations. From August 1977, North American market cars received a four-spoke wheel that was better able to spread loads in impact testing.

North American cars had inertia reel safety belts throughout the run, but inertia reels were only standardized on UK market Midget 1500s from April 1977. From August 1977 the instrument style package, but not the location, was changed, so that the Midget henceforth shared instruments with the Spitfire and the MGB.

PRODUCTION

Except for a tiny overlap, in September/October 1974 there was a clean handover at Abingdon between the end of BMC A-Series-engined Midget IIIs, and the start-up of Triumph-engined Midget 1500s. Visually, of course, the two cars were very different – the vast black bumpers of the new derivative making sure of that – but production methods were just the same as before.

The engine and transmission change meant that new supply chains had to be set up. Triumph engines were assembled at Radford in Coventry, while the all-synchromesh gearboxes (which were the same as those used in the Morris Marina) came from another Midlands-based British Leyland plant – both of them being of a basic type shared with the Spitfire 1500.

The start-up of production was brisk enough, for no fewer than 2,513 Midget 1500s were produced before the end of 1974 – 1,922 of them being des-

tined for North America. Production then increased briskly, to no fewer than 16,879 in 1976, before settling to more than 14,000 in each of the next two years. It was only in 1979, when the Midget was known to be under sentence of death (and when stocks of unsold cars were building up in North America), that production had to be reduced, and in fact the North American market model had almost disappeared by October 1979.

The last 500 UK market cars (chassis numbers 229001–229500) were painted black, and carried a 'fifty year' plaque on the facia panel, to celebrate the fact that the *original* M-Type Midgets had been built at Abingdon in 1929. The last Midget of all, also painted black, was produced on 7 December 1979, and was immediately delivered to the British Motor Industry Heritage Trust collection.

There were two other special-edition types. In mid-1975, a one-off 'Golden Jubilee' car was produced (to celebrate – wrongly – fifty years of the life of the MG marque) in New Racing Green with special badging and gold-tinted Rostyle wheels. Then, in mid-1976, for North America only there was a 'Midget Special', which carried special side stripes and was loaded with 'optional' equipment as standard, including a luggage rack.

CAREER

Compared with the complications of earlier Sprite/Midget models, this was a relatively simple model to describe. The Midget 1500 served only two markets – its own home territory and that of North America. Sales to other countries – in Europe or what we might call the old 'Empire' countries like Australia – had ceased with the Midget III. Ruthless or not, this was a policy of simplification, brought about by the sheer engineering, planning and assembly effort in building late-1970s cars for sale in North America.

With so much effort required to keep the Midget 1500 abreast of new North American

Did you ever need to ask what make of car this was? The famous MG octagon told its own story – the same badge, in every detail, that had graced Abingdon-built cars for half a century.

PRODUCTION	MG MIDGET 1500
DATES	November 1974–December 1979
CHASSIS NUMBERS	MIDGET: GAN6 154101–GAN6 229526
PRODUCTION BREAKPOINTS	March 1975: Introduction of Californian version (single carb. etc.) Oct. 1975: Introduction of 1976 USA model (single CD4T carb. etc.) Aug. 1977: 3.7:1 final drive ratio on all models.
TOTAL PRODUCED	72,289

- Black
- Pageant Blue
- Tahiti Blue
- Bracken
- Russet Brown
- Flamenco
- Harvest Gold
- Brooklands Green
- Carmine Red
- Damask Red

- Sandglow
- Tundra
- Vermilion
- Glacier White
- Leyland White
- Porcelain White
- Chartreuse Yellow
- Citron Yellow
- Inca Yellow

ACCESSORIES

- Head restraints
- Radio (USA only)
- Whitewall tyres (USA only)
- Wire-spoke wheels (to 1976, then dropped)

- Front anti-roll car kit
  (to 1977, then standard, all markets)
- Tonneau cover kit (USA only)
- Hardtop

At this time, BMC officially approved accessories included: windtone horns, luggage rack, fire extinguisher, reverse lamp, wing mirrors, child's seat, exhaust pipe trim, seat covers and other 'convenience' items.

crash-test, safety and exhaust emission regulations, there was little scope for mid-term facelifts, or indeed for any meaningful mechanical changes to be introduced in the life of the car. Although the late-1979 Midget 1500 was different in many details from the original late-1974 type, this was mainly forced upon the company by events.

A new steering wheel/instrument layout package (an obvious update) was introduced for North American market cars from August 1977. In addition, there was a constant drip-feed of minor changes, to lamps, to the position of instruments, to badging and to colour choices, meaning that there was really no obvious and visual Model Year break in the cars' run at Abingdon. Nevertheless, to meet rafts of new North American regulations (when packages of new details had to be introduced), the 1976 model cars (exhaust catalysts for all North American cars) started in October 1975, and the 1978 model cars (higher gearing, new North American steering wheel, new commonized instruments) started in August 1977.

The running down of all assembly started in October 1979 (there being no 1980 models to follow, nor export 'pipeline' to fill), and the last Midget 1500 of all was built on 7 December 1979.

RIVALS

In the late 1970s, as in the early 1970s (and the previous model), the Midget's main competition came from two cars – the Triumph Spitfire and the Fiat X1/9. The Spitfire, of course, was the in-house rival, and there are those who still do not know why this situation should have been allowed to persist.

No other cars truly broke in to this three-way battle for sales, neither in North America (the main arena), nor in Europe. Can the market really have been so restricted? It seems so, for a careful trawl through directories of the period confirms this. The pretty Italian-built Innocenti Spider, after all, had already disappeared, and the 1.3-litre and 1.6-litre Alfa Spiders were too large and a lot too expensive.

The main battle, of course, was between the Midget and the Spitfire, for although the Fiat X1/9 was an attractive little removable-roof coupe, it had no sporting heritage, and was already being damned with Fiat's 'rust away everyday' reputation. Not even an upgrade in 1978, to 1.5 litres and a five-speed transmission, could alter that.

As for the last twelve years, the Midget continued to square up to the Spitfire, this time on an almost level playing field, for the two cars shared

MG MIDGET 1500 (Basic North American market differences in square brackets)

ENGINE

Layout	Four cylinder, in-line
Block material	Cast iron
Head material	Cast iron
Peak power	66bhp (net) @ 5,500rpm [57bhp (net) @ 5,000rpm]
Peak torque	77lb.ft @ 3,000rpm [74b.ft @ 3,000rpm]
Bore	73.7mm
Stroke	87.5mm
Cubic capacity	1,493cc
Compression ratio	9.0:1 [7.5:1, except 1976]

FUEL SUPPLY

Carburettors	SU constant vacuum (Zenith–Stromberg constant vacuum]
Type	2 × HS4 [1 × CD4, later CD4T]
Fuel pump	AC Delco mechanical

ELECTRICAL

Earth	Negative
Battery	N9 12-volt
Generator	Lucas alternator
Starter motor	Lucas M35 J

TRANSMISSION

Clutch	Single-plate diaphragm spring
Clutch diameter	7¼in (18.5cm)
Gearbox type	Manual, four-speed, all-synchromesh
Internal ratios	4th: 1.00; 3rd: 1.433; 2nd: 2.119; 1st: 3.41; reverse: 3.753:1
Overall gear ratios	4th: 4.22; 3rd: 5.589; 2nd: 8.264; 1st: 13.299; reverse: 14.637:1

Note: From late 1977, the final drive ratio was changed from 3.9:1. to 3.7:1, this changing every intermediate ratio too.

BRAKES

Front, type	Lockheed disc, hydraulic
Front, size	8.25in diameter
Rear, type	Lockheed drum, hydraulic
Rear, size	7 × 1¼in

STEERING

Type	Rack and pinion
Turns (L–to–L)	2.75

Turning circle between kerbs	31ft 6in (9.6m) approx.

FRONT SUSPENSION

Type	Independent, coil springs, wishbones
Anti-roll bar	Standard
Dampers	Lever arm, hydraulic

REAR SUSPENSION

Type	Beam axle, half-elliptic leaf springs
Anti-roll bar	None
Dampers	Lever arm, hydraulic

WHEELS AND TYRES

Wheel size	13in diameter, 4½in rim width
Optional wire wheels	13in × 4.0in rim width
Tyres	Radial-ply
Tyre size	145-13in

CAPACITIES

Engine oil	8.0 pints
Gearbox oil	1.5 pints
Differential oil	1.75 pints
Cooling system	7.5 pints
Fuel tank	7 Imperial gallons [6.5 Imperial gallons]

DIMENSIONS

Length (with front bumper)	11ft 9in (3,580mm)
Width	4ft 5½in (1,360mm)
Height (unladen)	4ft 1¾in (1,260mm)
Wheelbase	6ft 8in (2,030mm
Front track	3ft 10½in (1,180mm)
Rear track	3ft 9in (1,140mm)
Ground clearance (unladen)	5in (127mm)
Weight (unladen)	1,700lb (771kg)

PERFORMANCE (UK market)

0–60mph (0–97kph)	12.3sec
Top speed	101mph (163kmh)
Standing ¼-mile	18.5sec
Overall fuel consumption	28mpg (10ltr/100km)
Typical fuel consumption	c.34mpg (c.8.3ltr/100km)

the same 1.5-litre engine and all-synchromesh gearbox assemblies – though they still sold through different dealer networks in North America. In UK market trim, both were 100mph cars, both had to use exactly the same type of 'detoxed' engines in North America, and both were increasingly lumbered with more weight as they had to beat ever-more demanding crash-test requirements.

Price levels were always to the Midget's advantage – just. In the USA, in 1975 the Midget sold for $3,549 compared with $3,745 for the Spitfire, the gap being wider in 1979 at $5,200 against $5,795.

In the UK, at the start of its run the Midget 1500 sold for £1,418, the Spitfire for £1,509 – and when the Midget disappeared at the end of 1979 it retailed for £3,604, when a Spitfire cost £4,064. This was the decade when the energy crisis, and subsequent inflation, hit car prices very hard indeed.

Throughout this period, honours were even, for the Midget outsold the Spitfire from 1974 to 1977, the Spitfire then winning the battle in 1978 and losing out again the following year. The Midget, of course, was discontinued at the end of 1979, the Spitfire struggling on for another year.

The Midget 1500 was built from late 1974 until the end of 1979. this being one of the very last cars to be produced. The polyurethane bumpers made the 1500 instantly recognizable.

OPPOSITE PAGE

TOP: In the mid- and late-1970s the Midget was available in an increasing variety of attractive colours, which partly made up for the lack of style changes to the structure itself. The 1500s, too, were not as low to the ground as earlier types.

BOTTOM: The addition of black polyurethane bumpers did the Midget's style no favours (other, less obtrusive ways could surely have been chosen), but the 1500 was still a neat, compact and appealing sports car – of which more than 100,000 were sold.

THIS PAGE

RIGHT: This Midget 1500's front bumper is polished to a standard probably not ever seen when such cars were newly assembled at Abingdon. Some owners do not like this fitting, and have had their cars recreated as 'chrome bumper' types.

So few sports cars still look good with the soft-top erect, but the Midget 1500 made it, somehow. There was plenty of all-round visibility, and those wind-up windows help keep out the wind.

OPPOSITE PAGE

Compared with the previous Midgets built from 1966–74, the 1500's rear aspect was unchanged. No '1500' badge was ever carried – though the black-bumper style told its own story. The chrome luggage rack is a period accessory fitment.

THIS PAGE

TOP: Reversing lights were, of course, standard on the Midget 1500.

BOTTOM: Several different types of steering wheel were fitted to Midget 1500s, this one having satin-finish alloy spokes. Note the neatly detailed home market facia/instrument layout.

THIS PAGE

ABOVE: Head rests (more officially known as 'head restraints') were necessary to meet certain North American crash-test regulations, but on the Spitfire 1500 they were standard for all sales markets including the UK.

The radio installation was as recommended by the factory, though a radio was never standard.

OPPOSITE PAGE

MAIN PICTURE: Neat, unobtrusive, effective – swivelling front quarter windows ahead of the wind-up glass of a Midget 1500's doors. Door mirrors were standard on the driver's side, but not always on the passenger side.

INSET: Neat and tidy interior door release handles, engineered to make sure that they were well clear of a passenger's limbs in the case of an accident.

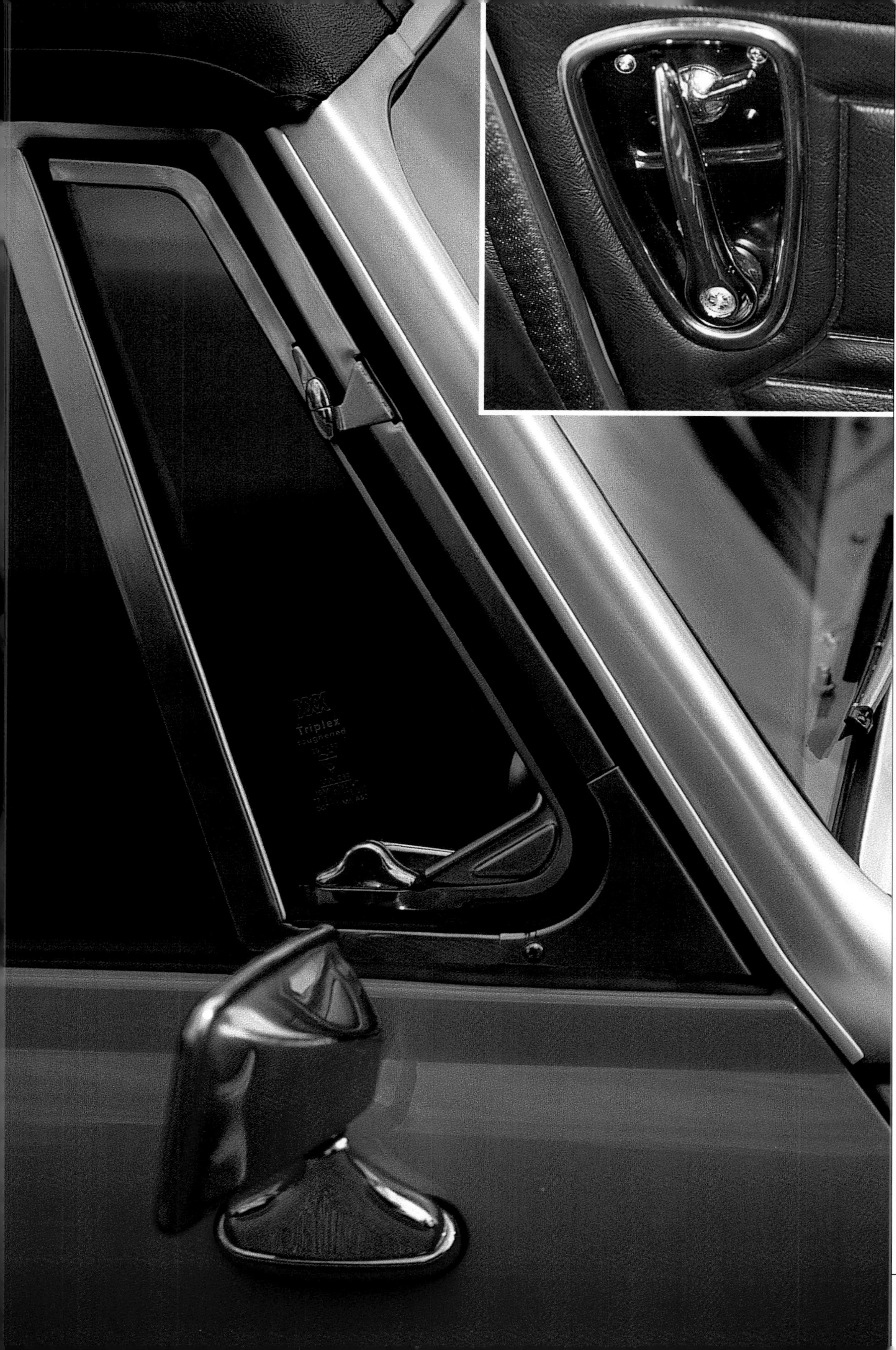
Triplex
toughened

OPPOSITE PAGE

TOP: Many feel that the Midget 1500's rear style, complete with 'black bumper', was at least the equal of the chrome-bumper type that had gone before.

BOTTOM: British Leyland never had the capital investment, nor the time, to spare to have the Midget's rear-end style totally integrated, so the reverse lamps were not incorporated into the tail lamp clusters, and the fuel filler was never hidden away under a flap.

THIS PAGE

TOP: The Midget 1500's boot was useful in shape, but quite small, and any luggage had to share space with the spare wheel (for which there was no cover) and the realigned fuel filler hose.

BOTTOM: The Midget 1500's sill badges were exactly the same as those used on earlier models in the 1970s.

When black polyurethane bumpers had to be fitted, British Leyland's stylists very sensibly decided to eliminate a separate grille altogether, so that cooling air reached the radiator of the 1500 through a simple 'black hole'.

All Midget 1500s were fitted with Rostyle wheels as standard, the same type as fitted to late-model Midget Mk IIIs in the early 1970s.

CHAPTER SEVEN

Replicas

DONALD and Geoff Healey did not like plagiarists, dilettantes and anyone who was not truly serious about their calling. This explains, no doubt, why they spent many years resisting those who wanted to deviate from the original layouts and recreate Austin-Healeys according to their personal inclinations – until the mid-1980s, that is, when Austin-Healey enthusiast Keith Brading started developing a completely new type of sports car on the Isle of Wight. It looked exactly like the original Frogeye Sprite, but was almost totally different under the skin.

Although the new car's engineering had good credentials – the separate, multi-tubular, chassis was developed by John Ackroyd (of Thrust II Land Speed Record design fame) – it was by no means as 'pure' a design as the original had been, for the latest type of A-Series engine (the 1,275cc version) was blended with original-style Sprite front suspension, a trailing-arm-type rear end with suspension by rubber in torsion, and a glass-fibre lookalike body.

Brading made sure that *his* car had no obvious visual failings, took care to get the prototype right, proposed to call it Frogeye (not an Austin-Healey) and finally convinced the Healey family that it was a worthy recreation/replica of what

they had designed thirty years earlier. To make sure that Brading did not deviate from that standard, Geoff Healey became an engineering consultant to the Frogeye Car Company, holding that position until his untimely death in 1994.

On sale from the start of the 1990s, it had modest success in the UK market, and was also unexpectedly popular in Japan, where a liking for 'traditional British' goods was well-established. From 1997, to make it faster, and more in tune with modern traffic conditions, the Frogeye was re-engineered to use a 102bhp/1.4-litre/16-valve Rover K-Series engine (the smaller version of that being employed in the MG MGF of the period), though the styling was not changed. However, sales continued to be slow, and the Frogeye project did not survive the 1990s.

While making it absolutely clear that the Frogeye is/was *not* an Austin-Healey, the fact that Geoff Healey approved of it, and that it has kept so much of the character, means that we should analyse it briefly, in the same way as the authentic cars. Note, however, that some 1958–61 Sprites have been recreated in a half-and-half manner, by utilizing a Frogeye chassis and body assembly, all the pieces from an otherwise rusted-out wreck of an original, and put on the road again.

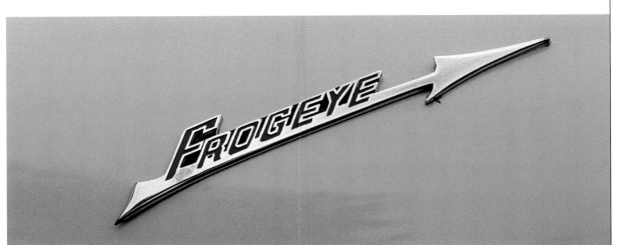

Attention to detail – the 'Frogeye' script of the replica was to the same style as 'Sprite' on the original cars.

STRUCTURE

The Frogeye took shape around a multi-tube chassis frame, with square-section tubes, one which incorporated the same front chassis legs as the original monocoque and the same type of solid front suspension/steering cross member. With sturdy sill tubes, and four tubes passing down the centre of the car from front cross member to what was effectively a rear backbone, this meant that the transmission tunnel had to be more bulky than the original.

All the suspension loads, and of course the engine and transmission, were fixed to this frame, which meant that the rest of the body shell (in glass-fibre) could be less solid.

BODY SHELL

The Frogeye was unique, in that it had a separate glass-fibre shell, to which every possible original Austin-Healey Sprite part – windscreen, sliding side-screens, soft-top, headlamps, wipers, front grille and tail lamps, even the original bonnet lifting handle, for instance – could be fixed in its original position.

Compared with the original steel shell and its layout, there was one big advance – the bonnet lift had been arranged so that it was now hinged at the front, and lifted forwards. Access to parts of the engine bay was better than before, though on the downside it was no longer as easy to get at the front suspension, steering and radiator/cooling areas.

As with the original 'real' car, there was a simple fascia/instrument panel with original-type instruments, though a more modern three-alloy spoke steering wheel was fitted. In many cases, it has to be admitted, the panel fit was better in the 1990s recreation than ever it had been when this shape of Sprite was new.

RUNNING GEAR

On the original cars, the main casings were almost entirely 'as you were' Sprite Mk I, though the chosen engine was now the later 1,275cc unit, the gear ratios were the later close ratio, while the final drive ratio was the original 4.22:1. However, sometimes, this was not the case – for also in the early days Brading could sometimes be persuaded to supply incomplete cars to which a customer would provide his own running gear, probably from a Sprite or cantilever-spring Midget that he was scrapping due to the monocoque being totally rusted out!

As production progressed, during the 1990s the specification became more and more unique to the Frogeye, and not at all like the original. From 1997, as already noted, the 'standard' engine became the 1.4-litre/16-valve K-Series unit, there was a five-speed (Ford-type) transmission, and the overall gearing was also changed.

SUSPENSION, STEERING AND BRAKES

Original cars had Sprite-type front suspension, with lever arm dampers which also doubled as top wishbones, but later in the 1990s this system was changed to double wishbones with telescopic dampers. The rear suspension, too, was modified from rubber-in-torsion, to become more conventional in its layout.

Unlike the original Sprite Mk Is, the Frogeye always had front-wheel disc brakes, which gave braking at least up to late-model Midget standards.

Wheels on original cars were current-model Sprite/Midget (some cars were supplied with wire-spoke wheels), but by the early 1990s the cars were also available with a lookalike type of Minilite seven-spoke alloy in cast aluminium.

COCKPIT AND TRIM

At a casual glance, this car could be an original Frogeye Sprite, except that the finish was better and the standard of equipment higher. Many owners fitted original Sprite pieces from their old cars anyway, and in more recent years a number had after-market carpets and sound-deadening equipment added.

The same type of 'build it yourself' soft-top/hood arrangement was retained, and was matched by sliding plastic side-screens.

PRODUCTION AND CAREER

The first cars were built c.1990, and the last in 1998–99. One sales problem (as with the Naylor TF1700, which was a lookalike of the original MG TF) was that the recreation was expensive. The first cars retailed for between £12,000 and £14,000, depending on what extras or options were fitted. Although they are rare in the UK, they seem to be well regarded. Naturally there were no style changes during this time.

OPPOSITE PAGE

TOP: Well-kept original Sprite? No, not at all – this is a nicely built Frogeye replica, which went on sale in 1990, with a separate tubular chassis and a glass-fibre body shell.

BOTTOM: There were very few visual differences between the Frogeye replica and the original Frogeye Sprite – this particular car of course having special alloy wheels to confuse everyone.

TOP: Right from every angle – even down to having the original bonnet-lifting handle in place (though it was not needed) – the replica Frogeye brought late-1950s sports car motoring back to 1990s enthusiasts (and rust-free, too).

BOTTOM: The one big difference between the Frogeye replica (this car) and an original Sprite, was that the bonnet assembly now hinged forward from the nose, making some (but not all) of the engine bay easier to service than before.

THIS PAGE

RIGHT: This was the access granted to the engine bay of the Frogeye replica, where the bonnet swung up and forwards, away from the bulkhead.

BELOW: The engine bay fittings of the Frogeye replica were repositioned compared with the original cars – the battery being off to one side, for instance with a cooling system header tank behind the engine. This car's A-Series engine has a special tappet cover and accessory-type carburettor filters.

ABOVE: On a Frogeye replica, this discreet badge, placed on the fascia panel ahead of the passenger's eyes, is important, for it signifies that Geoff Healey had given his approval to Keith Brading's way of recreating a 1950s original.

LEFT: In the 1970s, these Frogeye replica wheels would have been called Minilites, but when that company closed down, several lookalike wheels followed – these were by Minator.

BELOW: The Frogeye replica fascia/driver's display looks exactly like so many original-type Sprites, for owners often fitted alloy-spoked wheels with wooden rims, just like this.

Epilogue

BEFORE the formation of British Leyland in 1968, there were high hopes of seeing a replacement Sprite/Midget model developed, but these soon faded away. Triumph, rather than MG, soon became the corporation's favourite sports car, and Abingdon's enterprise was sidelined.

Here and there, along the way, there were false starts. Abingdon had wanted to go ahead with the Pininfarina-styled EX234 in the late 1960s, but that was killed off in 1968. Once the ADO 70 (a front-wheel drive Mini-based sports coupe which originated at Longbridge in the early 1970s) had also been abandoned, there was no hope. The choice of a Triumph Spitfire engine to power the Midget 1500 signalled the end.

Several factors then conspired to kill off the long-running line of sports cars from MG – notably the North American situation, the lack of progress on the style and performance front and British Leyland's finances. The state of the North American marketplace, and the cost of keeping cars abreast of the ever-changing and intensifying safety and exhaust emission regulations was critical. British Leyland (and the design team at Abingdon) found this task so demanding that there was neither the time, nor the financial resources, to devote to evolving a new model.

This therefore meant that the existing car, whose style basically dated from the launch of the Midget in 1961, could not be significantly changed. In the mid- and late-1970s, people who wanted to own a Midget were faced with buying a new car that had progressed very little for a decade – neither in performance nor in looks – and they began to look elsewhere. Because of this, sales peaked and began to ebb away (they were never as high as in the 1960s in any case), Abingdon was no longer as busy as before, and the profits of the 1960s turned into losses. Heavy UK inflation, which caused prices to soar, did not help.

To an accountant (though not to an MG enthusiast, whose priorities were entirely different), the only proper business decision was to wind up the project, bringing production to a close, and to clear the stocks. The rundown occurred in the autumn of 1979, and the last-ever Midgets were delivered in the USA, from stock, in 1980.

NO SUCCESSION

Embittered MG fans not only saw the Midget dropped, but then the MGB followed it a year later – and nothing came along to replace these cars. They must have smiled, though, when it became clear that the Triumph marque, too, was dying away, with the last Spitfire being produced in 1980, followed by the last of the TR7/TR8 family in 1981.

MG lived on throughout the 1980s, on a series of badge-engineered Austin-Rover cars such as the MG Metro, the MG Maestro and the MG Montego, which sold in big numbers but were not sporty cars. A change of company ownership combined with a change of marketing emphasis saw a much-modified and revised version of the MGB, the R V8, relaunched in 1992. However, except in the Japanese market, it was a commercial failure, although this was only a holding manoeuvre.

Finally, in 1995, Rover (which is what British Leyland had become, after a long and traumatic series of corporate changes) introduced the new MGF sports car, a two-seater with a transverse mid-engine driving the rear wheels. Although it was by no means 'Midget' – it was larger, more powerful and of course a lot more expensive (the first 118bhp/1.8-litre MGFs sold for £15,995) – the MGF was a genuine successor to the sort of Midget which had once been so popular.

MGF sales, once established, went ahead at the rate of approximately 10,000 cars a year, and even though Rover was rather insensitively dumped by its then owners, BMW, in 2000, the MGF continued to be improved as the 2000s opened. The company's new owners, in fact, then proposed to bring back the 'MG' badge to even more commercial importance than before, leaving everyone to assume that more MG sports car variety would follow in future years.

Index

References to Abingdon, Austin-Healey, BMC, British Leyland, MG, and their related models, are so frequent that these have not been separately indexed.